Under One Steeple

The House of Prisca and Aquila

OUR MISSION AT THE HOUSE OF PRISCA AND AQUILA IS TO PRODUCE QUALITY BOOKS that expound accurately the word of God to empower women and men to minister together in a multicultural church. Our writers have a positive view of the Bible as God's revelation that affects both thoughts and words, so it is plenary, historically accurate, and consistent in itself; fully reliable; and authoritative as God's revelation. Because God is true, God's revelation is true, inclusive to men and women and speaking to a multicultural church, wherein all the diversity of the church is represented within the parameters of egalitarianism and inerrancy.

The word of God is what we are expounding, thereby empowering women and men to minister together in all levels of the church and home. The reason we say women and men together is because that is the model of Prisca and Aquila, ministering together to another member of the church—Apollos: "Having heard Apollos, Priscilla and Aquila took him aside and more accurately expounded to him the Way of God" (Acts 18:26). True exposition, like true religion, is by no means boring—it is fascinating. Books that reveal and expound God's true nature "burn within us" as they elucidate the Scripture and apply it to our lives.

This was the experience of the disciples who heard Jesus on the road to Emmaus: "Were not our hearts burning while Jesus was talking to us on the road, while he was opening the scriptures to us?" (Luke 24:32). We are hoping to create the classics of tomorrow: significant and accessible trade and academic books that "burn within us."

Our "house" is like the home to which Prisca and Aquila no doubt brought Apollos as they took him aside. It is like the home in Emmaus where Jesus stopped to break bread and reveal his presence. It is like the house built on the rock of obedience to Jesus (Matt 7:24). Our "house," as a euphemism for our publishing team, is a home where truth is shared and Jesus' Spirit breaks bread with us, nourishing all of us with his bounty of truth.

We are delighted to work together with Wipf and Stock in this series and welcome submissions on a wide variety of topics from an egalitarian, inerrantist, global perspective.

For more information, visit www.houseofpriscaandaquila.com.

"*Under One Steeple* is must-reading for any church sharing or planning to share space with another church or churches . . . Anderson, drawing on twenty years of experience in what she calls 'hospiradicality' (Christ's radical hospitality), helps readers adopt a positive attitude toward sharing, while giving much practical advice. *Under One Steeple* is written in a conversational and devotional style that stretches our tolerance of others for the sake of Christ's love."

AÍDA BESANÇON SPENCER
Professor of New Testament
Gordon-Conwell Theological Seminary

"Lorraine Anderson brings the same openness and welcoming spirit to her book as she does to the groups that come inquiring about space at International Community Church. She brings an honest 'counting the cost' thoroughness to the challenge of shared space, with carefully thought-out forms and covenants at the back of the book, and yet a new vocabulary for working together . . . I heartily recommend [this book]!"

JUDY HALL
Assistant to the President
Emmanuel Gospel Center
Boston, Massachusetts

"Lorraine Anderson as much as any pastor I know in Boston has demonstrated not only unending generosity in sharing church space with other congregations and Christian ministries over many years, but she has also constantly demonstrated the skills and attentiveness required for ongoing, everybody-benefits kind of ways. Read this book-it's a must-read for all who believe God wants us to share the facilities he gives us."

RALPH KEE
Founder
Greater Boston Church Planting Collaborative

Under One Steeple

*Multiple Congregations
Sharing More Than Just Space*

LORRAINE CLEAVES ANDERSON

WIPF & STOCK · Eugene, Oregon

UNDER ONE STEEPLE
Multiple Congregations Sharing More Than Just Space

Copyright © 2012 Lorraine Cleaves Anderson. All rights reserved. Except for brief quotations in critical publications or reviews, no part of this book may be reproduced in any manner without prior written permission from the publisher. Write: Permissions, Wipf and Stock Publishers, 199 W. 8th Ave., Suite 3, Eugene, OR 97401.

Wipf & Stock
An Imprint of Wipf and Stock Publishers
199 W. 8th Ave., Suite 3
Eugene, OR 97401
www.wipfandstock.com

ISBN 13: 978-1-62032-011-2
Manufactured in the U.S.A.

Bagel image (chapter 1) by Gary Perlman, public domain, via Wikimedia.org.

Phone booth image (chapter 5) by Mattes, public domain, via Wikimedia.org.

Chair image (chapter 8) by Hannes Grobe, via Wikimedia.org.

Waving goodbye image (chapter 20) U. S. Navy photo by Photographer's Mate 2nd Class LaQuisha S. Davis, public domain, via Wikimedia.org.

Boat image (postscript) by Bernhard Suter, via Wikimedia.org.

All other photographs © 2011 by Rod Cleaves. All rights reserved.

Unless otherwise indicated, all Scripture quotations are taken from the Holy Bible, New Living Translation, copyright © 1996, 2004. Used by permission of Tyndale House Publishers, Inc., Carol Stream, Illinois, 60188. All rights reserved.

Poems in appendix C copyright © Jack Powers. Used by permission.

Under One Steeple is dedicated
with celestially dancing love to
Bob
Micah
Cara
Luke
Bethel
Cherith
Chris
Alisa

Jesus said, "For I was hungry, and you fed me. I was thirsty, and you gave me a drink. I was a stranger, and you invited me into your home. I was naked, and you gave me clothing. I was sick, and you cared for me. I was in prison, and you visited me." "Lord, when did we ever see you hungry and feed you? Or thirsty and give you something to drink? Or a stranger and show you hospitality? Or naked and give you clothing? When did we ever see you sick or in prison and visit you?" And the King will say, "I tell you the truth, when you did it to one of the least of these my brothers and sisters, you were doing it to me!"

(Matt 25:35, 36, 40)

Contents

A Song: Reciprocate *xi*
Acknowledgments xiii
Foreword xv
Preface xix

1 Scrutinize the "Hospiradical" Incarnation of Jesus 1
2 Pinpoint the Nonnegotiables 8
3 Welcome Every Knock on the Door, Every Ring of the Phone 16
4 Host Whole People Groups 22
5 Listen for God's Wisdom 28
6 Say "Yes" as Often as Possible 35
7 Carpe Occasionem 41
8 Count the Cost Gladly 47
9 Keep the Infrastructure as Self-Managing as Possible 54
10 Drop Negative Signs and Business Lingo 58
11 Have as Few Rules to Enforce as Possible 64
12 Set Grace-Plumped Boundaries, and Leave the Maturing to God 67
13 Take Prayerful Risks 73
14 Celebrate Cultural and Linguistic Distinctives 81
15 Start Peer Learning Groups 88

16　Hang World Maps and International Art　95

17　Pray! Pray! Pray!　101

18　Play! Play! Play!　108

19　Stay! Stay! Stay!　113

20　Leave Well　119

Postscript　125
Appendix A: Covenant for Shared Space　127
Appendix B: Covenant for Resident-Custodian　136
Appendix C: Poems by Jack Powers　139

A Song: *Reciprocate*

Sung to the tune of *Amazing Grace*

1. With soothing water, towel, and care,
    Friend, may I wash your feet?
    "Mine too are tired; so Lord, humble me
    To let her reciprocate."

2. With silent words and honest prayer,
    Friend, may I dry your tears?
    "Mine too are aflame; so Lord, humble me
    To let him reciprocate."

3. God's love for God—reciprocal.
    Friend, God loves you the same.
    "Lord, pour in your love and humble me
    That I may reciprocate."

4. With gratitude and heav'n-born joy
    Friends, may I step aside?
    "They've learned and prayed. Now Lord, humble me
    As they reciprocate."

By Lorraine Cleaves Anderson, © 2011.

Acknowledgments

WE ALL owe our unrivaled gratitude to the consummate Host of Hosts, in whose home there is always extra room.

I extend deepest thanks to the countless immigrants and church family who have allowed me a glimpse into their joys and heartbreaks, their cultures and experiences—especially my colleagues and friends, younger and older, from New Life Church and International Community Church (American Baptist) in Boston.

To Drs. Aída and Bill Spencer of House and Prisca and Aquila, I express warmest appreciation for considering this work as part of their esteemed series. I am humbled. To my friend and editor extraordinaire Deb Beatty Mel, whose gentle expertise is rainforest-rare, I offer sincere and rousing applause.

To Ralph and Judy Kee, who, many years ago, courageously put their careers on the line in support of my pastoral calling, words droop in articulating my very deepest respect and honor.

Lastly, to my buddy and my pal Bob, my patient beloved of three and a half decades, you are gold. And Luke, you will always be my treasure.

Agape galore,
Lorraine Cleaves Anderson

Foreword

THE OLDER, long-term members at "First" Church were frustrated. It was clear that their Northern European value system had been stretched to the breaking point by the immigrant Haitian congregation that had been meeting in "their" church building for some years. As a neutral third party representing the denomination, I tried to probe to find what was behind their anger. I didn't hold out much hope for a mutually agreeable, Christ-reflecting resolution. The Anglo congregation had already served an eviction notice, had extended it, had rescinded it, had some months later re-served it. The Haitian congregation had been exploring other options for meeting space, but all were substantially overpriced for their means. I know. I had gone with the pastor to check out about a dozen possibilities, only to have hopes dashed each time.

So I asked the question again: What was motivating the Anglo congregation to evict the Haitian congregation? I feared that it would be nothing other than racism, disguised. Hesitatingly, answers started to be articulated: some of the silk altar flowers were missing, some hymnals had crayon marks, the "rent" was in arrears, the Haitians used the church at hours other than those agreed upon, on some occasions the heat or lights were left on. . . . Was it racism coupled with a myopic view of the gospel or legitimate relationship-breaking issues? You can decide. Whichever, the

Haitians got the message loud and clear: *You are no longer welcome here!*

So, the Haitian congregation did eventually purchase a sanctuary in a different part of the city, and they have struggled under the payments and maintenance to the point where foreclosure is a distinct possibility. Meanwhile, the Anglo congregation lives in serenity, off their endowment, as each year the congregation shrinks. They are down to a couple of dozen elderly folk. The Haitians, though severely oppressed by the financial burden, average one hundred people in worship, have a vibrant youth group and outreach ministries, and have just started an English-language service in an effort to reach out to the non-Haitians in their new neighborhood!

Two ministries may close, one due to financial difficulties and the other to gospel deprivation. Why? Because Christians chose to act in ways that grieve Christ's heart. What if the Anglos viewed the Haitian church as God's outreach ministry? What if the Haitians had insisted on regular time of prayer and coordination across congregations? What if the Anglos had worked at their racism-denied? What if the Haitians had learned the trigger points of the dominant US culture and devised ways to avoid hitting them? What if both congregations had developed a covenantal relationship and worked at being responsible partners in the gospel? What if . . . ?

Certainly, one reason was inadequate motivation to attain that rigorous level of faithfulness to Christ's call. *But,* even if the motivation had been there, the means to achieve it would have been a mystery. How does one work toward a covenantal relationship across cultures? How does one attain high levels of trust, caring, and communication with people with some variance of values? How does one work through the inevitable bumps in the road? These two congregations had no roadmap to inform their journey toward these kingdom goals.

In the following pages, Rev. Lorraine Anderson provides this long-awaited roadmap. Multiple congregations sharing space, with Christ's love and kingdom goals at the center, is the face of the future for churches in the US. For those who wish to be so faithful, this roadmap is now available. Read it. Live it! And soon you will hear, "Well done, thou good and faithful servants!"

Anthony G. Pappas
Executive Minister,
The American Baptist Churches of Massachusetts
November 2011

Preface

He was homesick. Too many years had evaporated without holding his wife and child, and today he felt irritable and lonesome as he drove this gentleman to the doctor. His passenger was rambling on about nothing in particular, and Maung just wished for enough quiet to nurse his own brooding.

"Why aren't I transporting my own sisters, my own father and brother-in-law? Lord, why can't I be with my own family?"

The Holy Spirit whispered back:

"You *are* with your family. I have given you this man as your brother while you are away from home."

Instantly Maung's grief melted, and he thanked God for his radical ways, for bringing a family to him when he had no family nearby.

Our Lord is the consummate Host, offering to make his home in us and welcoming us into himself (John 14:23). As his followers, we find that unearthed treasures await when we act as hosts to both newly arrived immigrants and the ignored. It can take up to ten years, we're told, for an immigrant to settle adequately into our society. Meanwhile, we can welcome them Christianly and stand with them while they find their bearings.

Since God has blessed our church in hosting others for more than two decades, people are eager to share their similar experiences with us.

"We tried that, but it was a disaster! They left the kitchen in a greasy mess and the drains plugged . . . so we had to kick them out. Never again!"

"They were assigned the old nursery in the basement from 1:00 to 2:30, but they were still carrying on boisterously at 3:45. Neighbors could even hear their prayers across the street! Imagine! And their children jumped all over our parlor chairs that Mrs. Snaffit—may her soul rest in peace—donated forty years ago. One chair leg broke off and the slipcover tore right down the middle. We simply couldn't tolerate their disrespect. We had no choice but to cancel their contract and aren't about to rent to another church any time soon!"

Then I commiserate and tell them the five reasons why they should not "*rent*" space to another church:

1. Your trash cans will fill up with odiferous spices and your washrooms will need to be cleaned more often.
2. Things that are *disappearing around here* will show up in weird places.
3. You will constantly need to practice *carpe diem*, making your committees mad and exhausting yourselves.
4. People popping by to tell their stories will cut into your TV shows and disrupt your routine.
5. Their vitality will make your church look bad.

Then, I tell them five reasons why they should "*rent*" space to others:

1. Your trash cans will fill up with odiferous spices and your washrooms will need to be cleaned more often.
2. Things that are *disappearing around here* will show up in weird places.
3. You will constantly need to practice *carpe diem*, making your committees mad and exhausting yourselves.
4. People popping by to tell their stories will cut into your TV shows and disrupt your routine.
5. Their vitality will make your church look bad.

According to the *American Heritage Dictionary of the English Language*, "radical" is defined as "arising from or going to a root or source; fundamental; basic; extreme; sweeping; favoring or effecting revolutionary change." Sounds like Jesus. Furthermore, the term "hospitality" comes from "hospitable," and means "welcoming guests with warmth and generosity; well-disposed toward strangers." Thank God that when we were strangers wandering in sin, Jesus found us and took us in . . . whew!

Multiple congregations sharing just space smacks of one-dime, cheesy-cassette-recording-type hospitality. But multiple congregations *under one steeple* sharing more than just space thunders out a riches-in-Christ windfall, dancing-with-Jesus kind! Burdens lighten, joy erupts, and suddenly a great spiritual opus resounds in our soul from a not-your-everyday kind of hospitality, but a hospitality that is radical and rich and real, which could be called *hospiradicality*.

Hospitality is rooted in the notion of *home*. While it's true that "there is no place like home" (wistfully spoken by Dorothy in the film the *Wizard of Oz*), whole people groups find themselves dramatically displaced and scarred, often permanently. How do they pick up the pieces of their lives and go on? Do we look the other way and breathe a sigh of relief—"Well at least they're not my family"?

Or do we do our part, together, as members of the body of Christ, to offer a second church home under our own steeple, comforting the stranded, giving our best to our new friends and *living* the Bible, not just quoting it?

It's fun and it's a win/win for everyone!

It is my prayer and hope that readers of these true stories will launch into hosting congregations and ministries with a radical hospitality mirrored only in Jesus himself. May we continue discovering that, as a teacher learns more than her students, we need each other far more than we know, that we are repeatedly exhorted in Scripture to synthesize the rhizomatous love of Jesus, and that within collaborative ministry—sharing far more than just space—resides our laboratory.

Chapters are entitled with a vocative premise, championed in Scripture, robed in true narratives, capped with a slogan, and footed with biblical ponderings. Don't skip over the Scriptures, for in them are the vitamins for the journey. *Bon appétit!*

For any malapropisms, I apologize. Please put your feet up with a decadent cup of hot chocolate, adjust the lighting, and read with your heart, a tissue, and the dog.

Blessings galore,
Lorraine Cleaves Anderson
Boston, Massachusetts
July 2011

INITIAL SCRIPTURES TO PONDER

May God's peace be on this house. (Luke 10:5)

Jew and Gentile are the same in this respect. They have the same Lord, who gives generously to all who call on him. (Rom 10:12)

There is no longer Jew or Gentile, slave or free, male and female. For you are all one in Christ Jesus. (Gal 3:28)

1

Scrutinize the "Hospiradical" Incarnation of Jesus

*He came into the very world he created,
but the world didn't recognize him.*

—JOHN 1:10

A POET IN OUR MIDST

Smiling, Margaret arrived a few minutes into the service with another friend in tow, demonstrating the understated gregariousness we all love about her. He was tall, a bit eccentric, cheerful. He seemed delighted to meet new people and entered into the worship enthusiastically. As the sermon progressed, Jack hung on every word, occasionally even asking a question. He began attending every Bible study, retreat, dinner, worship, outreach, garden tending, and even started a Thursday night small group for fledgling poets. We gradually learned that he was a poet himself and an artist.

"That's nice."

He gave us one of his paintings of Jesus, which curiously resembled a self-portrait. It hung in the lobby where our rock show kids could view it, an artifact of much discussion, until one day it went missing, never to show up again.

Then, one day, he told me he wanted to be baptized in water. He'd been baptized—several times—but never by immersion.

"I want the gold, Cadillac version," he declared.

Well, I don't just *do* ceremonies . . . they have to be impregnated with a soul-deep meaning, so I probed Jack on his spiritual life and his relationship with the Messiah. Yes, indeed, he had invited Jesus into his life, had asked forgiveness for anything standing between God and himself, and intended to follow his Lord until God fetched him. The day of the baptism arrived, and, as usual, the water was breath-stealing icy. Margaret was my assistant.

"I baptize you, John Powers, in the name of the Father, and of the Son, and of the Holy Spirit. Amen."

I leaned him back in the baptismal tank with Margaret behind him, but he caught himself just before going under. We tried and coaxed and waited while Jack paced the baptismal tank, simply unable to go under the water.

Several minutes later, I said, "Jack, sit down on the steps here and we'll splash you royally."

So the assembled guests and congregation joined us in shouting, "In the name of the Father," splash, "and of the Son," splash, splash, "and of the Holy Spirit, Amen!" splash, splash, *splash*! Jack was drenched and thoroughly baptized into Christ's death and raised to new life!

Little by little, Jack's gait became more shuffling, his speech more halting. He spilled and dropped things more often. As it became more difficult for him to wrap his thoughts into words and sentences, people at ICC[1] were amazingly patient.

"Take your time, Jack. We're not in a hurry. Do you mean . . . ?"

Over the next several years, Jack grew less verbal. His familiar, "Okay!" morphed into his signature thumbs up and serious nod. We fretted with Margaret over his habit of impulsively walking out into the night, resisting all restraint, even for his own safety. Once he bolted, only to reappear with a hot pizza from across the street to serve to his church friends. Jack was thoughtful and affirming, with and without a voice.

---

1. An acronym for International Community Church—an American Baptist Church, 30 Gordon Street, Boston, MA, 02134.

As I became more familiar with some of his poetry and heard bits and pieces of his accomplishments, I wanted to honor him somehow. Coincidentally, his seventieth birthday loomed, so several of us planned a celebration. As the evening unfolded, I was perhaps the only person unprepared for the unfeigned accolades of the city's poetry community. By this time, Jack was essentially mute and seemed genuinely dumbfounded by all the attention, including that of his adult sons.

But it wasn't until he crossed the threshold into the waiting presence of his Lord that our church met the Jack whom everyone else had known for decades. The hum of his memorial service was that of voices catalyzed by their voiceless inspiriter. I remember telling everyone what Jesus meant to him:

"Jesus was Jack's kind of Guy, and Jack was Jesus'. Since we're a church that focuses on the Christ, maybe that's why Jack decided to hang around and let us love him. We never knew the Jack you are describing this morning. . . . God brought him here so that our little church could accompany him to heaven. And what an honor it has been."

Half a year later during National Poetry Month, a group of dozens of his friends and protégés returned to his church for a memorial poetry reading, honoring the life of their beloved Jack. Person after person, old and young alike, testified:

"I would not be the poet I am today had it not been for Jack."

"I never dreamed of singing in front of people until Jack cheered, 'Give it a go. You can do it!'"

Artists, poets, singers, instrumentalists, activists, seekers—all had found their voices because of Jack. Through his weekly open-mic forum at Stone Soup Poetry, he ministered to thousands who otherwise would have lived unfulfilled lives plagued by chronic ruminative indigestion.

We had no idea who was among us in the person of Jack Powers. Analogously, Jesus lived among his own family and friends, but they *didn't recognize him*.

Who else is sitting on the church steps?

THE MAN BEHIND THE BAGELS

On school days after dropping our son off at the T,[2] I would bop over to a bagel shop in Coolidge Corner, where many a sermon was scribbled on their napkins. It was a little piece of community in the middle of a bustling city. There was Tom who, in all his years of going there, never ate a bagel—Tom, the supposed lawyer, who turned out to be, in fact, a banker. There was Al, who owned a window treatment shop; Moise, who worked as a painter; and an overly friendly choir member always dressed in a suit and tie who could talk unfettered. Sandy who worked the register made everyone feel like royalty and was a major reason people kept coming back.

Then, there was this cute college student named Eric Bru whose charm translated into poppy seed bagels and chive cream cheese extraordinaire. He could mop a floor like a superhero, divvy out change like an Einstein, and slap tomatoes and mayo on garlic bagels with Julia Child finesse.

---

2. "The T" is local parlance for the Massachusetts Bay Transportation Authority's subways and buses.

Eric, too, created among customers a sense of camaraderie that was electric. He was applying to law schools, and we all cheered him on through his regular updates. When, as anticipated, he was accepted and would be leaving his minimum-wage job, we were elated for him, sad for us.

During the last week of his employment, customers swung by to say goodbye and wish him well. No one was prepared for *his* farewell to all of us. He had created a new nametag for himself, which, when the regulars read it, caused smelling salts to appear. With an arresting grin and polar-bear hugs, he told customers one after another,

"I'm Eric Bruegger!"

"What? I thought you were Eric Bru! You're joking, right?"

He was, in fact, the owner's son. Bruegger's Bagels.

Analogous to Jesus' incarnation, Eric *came into the very [business his father] created, but [neither the staff nor the customers] recognize[d] him*. He had practiced radical hospitality among his peers and customers.

Yet again, the world teaches the church how to love.

> *God embodied himself in Jesus, bringing his hospitality directly to this world, and now extends a hospitable hand to draw you into his heart. Why not take him up on it and let him embrace you? Come home to Jesus, for more of his radical hospitality awaits when you cross the threshold to live in his eternal home forever!*

ADDITIONAL SCRIPTURES TO PONDER ON THE "HOSPIRADICAL" INCARNATION OF JESUS

Look! The virgin will conceive a child! She will give birth to a son, and they will call him Immanuel, which means "God is with us." (Matt 1:23)

Then Jesus said, "Come to me, all of you who are weary and carry heavy burdens, and I will give you rest. Take my yoke upon you. Let me teach you, because I am humble and gentle at heart, and you will find rest for your souls. For my yoke is easy to bear, and the burden I give you is light." (Matt 11:28–30)

Be sure of this, I [Jesus] am with you always, even to the end of the age. (Matt 28:20)

Jesus said, "Look! I stand at the door and knock. If you hear my voice and open the door, I will come in, and we will share a meal together as friends." (Rev 3:20)

2

Pinpoint the Nonnegotiables

Simon Peter replied, "Lord, to whom would we go? You have the words that give eternal life. We believe, and we know you are the Holy One of God."

—JOHN 6:68–69

A VISIT FROM A NEIGHBOR

At ICC, we uphold three nonnegotiables: a high view of

1. The person and work of Jesus Christ,
2. The two greatest commandments, according to Jesus, and
3. The authority of Scripture.

Period.

I just happened to be updating the master calendar when the doorbell rang.

"Hello! May I help you?"

"I've passed by many times and wanted to drop in to see your building. Do you rent space for family gatherings?"

When I'm alone in the building, I welcome male strangers cautiously, generally stepping outside to converse. But this time, others were coming in and out.

"Come in and let's talk. Tell me what you have in mind."

We strolled through the children's room, through the little chapel, and into the auditorium where some volunteers had just painted a huge mural of the face of Jesus laughing on one imposing, blank wall, inspired by the artwork of Ralph Kozak. It depicted what I'd been imagining for years: a visual of Jesus' love for our rock-show young people, just as they are. Only his love—not his scowl—can attract them to him.

"That big room would be perfect. I'm looking for a place for my family and friends to enjoy our culture with all its festivities. We only need space for four or five hours, and we'll be sure to clean up carefully. How much do you charge?"

"Tell me a little more about the party you're planning."

"Well, we will have lots of traditional food, music, and dance. Maybe you can come! The children, of course, need space to play . . . but don't worry, we'll supervise them well. We will set up candles and our gods, then we will eat and dance, and basically have a great time being together. We can't seem to find any place that will allow us to honor our culture and worship our gods."

"Hmmm. I see. That big painting in there . . . that's an artist's idea of what God's Son Jesus *may* have looked like. We don't bow down to that picture. It just reminds us how real he is and how profoundly he loves all of us, including you! Then as we strive to follow in his footsteps, we find ourselves remarkably changed and in relationship with the living God. Yikes, spikes! Jesus is right here with us now, but not on that wall!"

"I didn't know that. I thought Christians worshipped their pictures and statues."

"Nope. At least we don't here. Drawings and wood carvings and plaster of Paris only represent the living, invisible God who can't be contained in a picture or figurine. In fact, the Bible cautions us about bowing down to any gods other than the Lord of Lords, the King of all Kings.

"I'm so sorry, but we can't set up your gods here. It is exactly opposite to what we read in God's word, the Bible. But please, if you would like to have a birthday party or other gathering for your family and friends, we'd be delighted to have you. We just can't allow the worship of other gods here. I hope you understand."

"Oh yes. In fact, my children should learn the stories about this Jesus since they live in America now."

"We tell the stories every Sunday morning, and this summer we'll be having a whole week of After-Supper Bible Camp. Your kids would have a blast! Here, take my card and stay in touch."

With that, he was off. I missed an opportunity in forgetting to get his name and contact information. I've never seen him again, but so hope he felt welcomed, not disrespected; heard, not criticized. If his ten minutes inside a Christian house of worship, where Jesus and his word are honored, was, at the least, hospitable, it was enough . . . for now.

MISLEADING MESSAGES

The heading contained the words "family values," and, since I'm always looking for ways to strengthen marriages and families around here, I read their flier. It sounded solid, contained endorsements by Reverend this and Bishop that, so I sent back the card requesting more information. Mistake number one.

A week or so later, two women appeared at the door, fists full of literature, eager to explain their program. We chatted, and I invited them to church. Sure enough, the next Sunday they showed up. Terrific! They stayed for tea, mingled, and I thought that was that. Mistake number two.

More mailings arrived. No red flags jumped out from their promotional material; however, this time I examined the vaguely familiar return address with a sickening wave of nausea.

"Oh, no."

Immediately, I dialed the number to inquire about their supporting organization. As I expected, the receptionist was evasive. A few days later, the two women returned: obviously foreigners in their mid-twenties. This time, I invited them in with grave concern, knowing they had been meticulously trained to respond to the likes of me.

"I know the organization you work for. Listen to me. They are teaching you lies. Here in the Holy Bible it says:

> Jesus told them, "Don't let anyone mislead you, for many will come in my name, claiming, 'I am the Messiah.' They will deceive many. . . . And many false prophets will appear and will deceive many people. . . .
>
> "Then if anyone tells you, 'Look, here is the Messiah,' or 'There he is,' don't believe it. For false messiahs and false prophets will rise up and perform great signs and wonders so as to deceive, if possible, even God's chosen ones. See, I have warned you about this ahead of time.
>
> "So if someone tells you, 'Look, the Messiah is out in the desert,' don't bother to go and look. Or, 'Look, he is hiding here,' don't believe it!" (Matthew 24:4, 5, 11, 23–25)

"You are in danger by believing what they're telling you. Here, take this booklet."

I gave them the little purple *Who's Jesus?*, well written by Alpha USA, along with a couple of other pamphlets, and prayed with them. They didn't refute my claims; in fact, their faces were crestfallen. A hopeful sign, I thought.

"Lord, please do penetrate their minds and souls and rescue them from the clutches of this group."

Different women showed up at the church a week or so later, this time three, not two. "Fresh troops," I mused. I told them please not to come back and to remove our name from their mailing list.

More mailings came. I called their headquarters and asked them please to delete us from their lists.

"Of course."

More mail, not only to ICC, but also addressed now to all the churches in our building. I tore them up and called again. My voice was stern.

"I have called numerous times to ask you politely to remove our churches and address from your mailing lists. We do not want your mailings or your visits any more."

"Oh, sorry. I'll take care of it right away. Thank you."

Two more women rang the doorbell a couple of weeks later. In no uncertain terms, I reiterated my demand—not request:

"Stay away. Don't come back!"

I felt terrible for these younger adults, embroiled in a philoso-theology that was destructive. But, as senior pastor, I had to protect our sheep, including the congregations we hosted.

When the mailings still did not subside, I called again—only this time, I threatened to take out a restraining order against them if they did not leave us alone. I called other churches and ministries to warn them of their mass mailings and continued praying.

Finally, they stopped coming to our church and their mailings desisted. Shortly thereafter, I saw a two-page spread in the *Boston Globe* advertising their upcoming event being held in a major downtown hotel. The one true messiah himself, it proclaimed, would be speaking for the last time ever in the United States. If we wanted stronger families in this life and eternal life in the next, we must come to hear in person the Reverend Sun Myung Moon.

Nausea flooded me again.

Everything's about Him, you know.[1]

ADDITIONAL SCRIPTURES TO PONDER ON CHRISTO-BIBLIO-CENTRICITY

Your word is a lamp to guide my feet and a light for my path. (Ps 119:105)

Because of that experience, we have even greater confidence in the message proclaimed by the prophets. You must pay close attention to what they wrote, for their words are like a lamp shining in a dark place—until the Day dawns, and Christ the Morning Star shines in your hearts. Above all, you must realize that no prophecy in Scripture ever came from the prophet's own understanding, or from human initiative. No, those prophets were moved by the Holy Spirit, and they spoke from God. (2 Pet 1:19–21)

Have I been with you all this time, Philip, and yet you still don't know who I am? Anyone who has seen me has seen the Father! . . . Just believe that I am in the Father and the Father is in me. (John 14:9, 11)

Christ is the visible image of the invisible God. He existed before anything was created and is supreme over all creation, for through him God created everything

---

1. Young, *The Shack*, 191.

Pinpoint the Nonnegotiables 15

> in the heavenly realms and on earth. He made the things we can see and the things we can't see—such as thrones, kingdoms, rulers, and authorities in the unseen world. Everything was created through him and for him. He existed before anything else, and he holds all creation together. (Col 1:15–17)

> For in Christ lives all the fullness of God in a human body. (Col 2:9)

> To the Son he says, "Your throne, O God, endures forever and ever. You rule with a scepter of justice." (Heb 1:3, 8)

> For the word of God is alive and powerful. It is sharper than the sharpest two-edged sword, cutting between soul and spirit, between joint and marrow. It exposes our innermost thoughts and desires. Nothing in all creation is hidden from God. Everything is naked and exposed before his eyes, and he is the one to whom we are accountable. So then, since we have a great High Priest who has entered heaven, Jesus the Son of God, let us hold firmly to what we believe. (Heb 4:12–14)

> Then I looked again, and I heard the voices of thousands and millions of angels around the throne and of the living beings and the elders. And they sang in a mighty chorus: "Worthy is the Lamb who was slaughtered—to receive power and riches and wisdom and strength and honor and glory and blessing." (Rev 5:11–12)

3

Welcome Every Knock on the Door, Every Ring of the Phone

As Jesus was saying this, the leader of a synagogue came and knelt before him. "My daughter has just died," he said, "but you can bring her back to life again if you just come and lay your hand on her." So Jesus and his disciples got up and went with him. Just then a woman who had suffered for twelve years with constant bleeding came up behind him.

—MATTHEW 9:18–20

SURPRISE SERENADE

Larry sat nervously in the little chapel as Margaret hustled to the second floor restroom to get dressed. It was the day after Easter. Their private wedding was scheduled for 2:00 p.m. with just the two of them, one of our residents to take photos, and me—but the bride was immobilized over her nuptial trousseau.

"Should I wear the blue top or this white one? I like this one, but I forgot to bring a skirt. I only have this slip."

I actually thought she looked stunning in the nylon slip and white sequined top.

Just then, the doorbell rang, so I hustled down to greet the cutest young man ever, standing at the glass door with a delightful smile and a violin case in his hand.

"Hello! Come in!"

"I'm a Boston University student and am looking for a place to hold my spring recital. Might it be possible to have it here?" It was now 1:50 p.m.

"Anything's possible. Actually, we're about to start a private wedding ceremony, but it's going to be slightly delayed, so let's chat a little now. What date are you considering?"

"Next month. Do you have a piano?"

"Sure. In the sanctuary."

"Would it be all right if I just took a quick peek at it? I'll only be a moment."

While the most adorable, sneaker-footed young man in Boston shyly went to check out the piano and tune his violin, I scampered back upstairs to see how our bride was faring. She was still statuesque in her slip. She asked if I would run out to her car to retrieve a certain blue-green skirt tucked down inside a grocery bag. As I darted down the stairs, up wafted the most heavenly music ever.

When I arrived back with the prize skirt in hand, Margaret wistfully noted,

"That's my favorite piece! Chopin's number . . ." something or other.

"Really? Hold on." I flew down the stairs to the sweet boy–young adult and asked, "By any chance, could you stay a few more minutes and play this number for the bride as she enters the sanctuary?"

"Well, I have class at 3:00 p.m., but okay, I can stay a little longer."

At approximately 2:35 p.m., the bride entered at the back of the church looking positively radiant in her white sequined blouse and blue-green skirt, regally escorted by her invisible Lord. Clutching a delicate bouquet, she looked alternately into her groom's misty eyes, then into the distance, as the strains of Chopin saturated the air.

Following several opening comments, I turned to our musician and asked,

"Would you by any chance have a violin number you could play for the bride and groom?"

And play he did, with all his heart. Romantic. Elegant. Perfect. Then he said simply,

"Congratulations! I hope you will be very happy. I have to go now." And he disappeared as quickly as he had come. It was 2:50 p.m.

Had we been visited by an angel? Thank You, God, for that doorbell ring.

A WELCOME ADDITION OF YOUTHFUL ENERGY

When we first began meeting in the building, I would try to work there, but found myself stifled and overcome. I'd pick up the phone and dial my colleague.

"Judy. I can't stand it in here. It smells musty, everything's brown and old, and I can't concentrate!"

"Open the windows! Turn the music up loud! Prance through the rooms singing and praying—you'll feel better!"

So I did, and she was right. Little by little, we cheered things up, hung brightly colored artwork, and began to hear laughter and conversation. Then, one day, the phone rang.

"I'm from the Boys and Girls Club nearby and we need a place to continue our programming while our facility undergoes major renovation. Any chance . . . ?"

"Come on over so we can meet each other and talk."

Alex was a buoyant man with a spirit the size of Jupiter. I guess as a Christian himself, he thought housing the club in a church just might have some osmotic effect on the kids. The alternative public high school that had used our basement for a decade had recently closed, so we did, in fact, have space, albeit more limited than their soon-to-be-state-of-the-art Boys and Girls Club.

"Oh no, it's perfect. We don't need a lot of room since we'll only be here about a year—so if your leaders approve, we'd love to join you. And note that the city will pay a handsome rent [quickly I thanked him and told him we didn't use that word anymore] and will hire a professional cleaning service for both our rooms and the rest of the building three times a week."

Gulp. How could we turn down an offer like that? We didn't. Come fall, the place was hopping with energetic kids and teens and enthusiastic staff, with gratitude oozing from every encounter. We had scored a win, realizing much-appreciated revenue plus youthful vigor and life. Somehow even the air smelled fresher!

When construction took a bit longer than anticipated, some of them became a little antsy, while we were ecstatic! We had come to know the staff well, had meaningful exchanges, knew many of the kids, and had grown fond of each other overall. When they did finally move into their new property, many expressed nostalgia for the close quarters and warm ambiance of the church.

"Thank You, God, for that."

Their extended stay seeped into the fall and would take them through Christmas. But that particular academic year got off to a turbulent start. Ever so many one-on-one chats around that time puckered the hours. Although they were a nonreligious, city-funded outreach to kids, some of their staff found themselves sitting in the sanctuary one afternoon, , some crying softly, faces solemn and fearful. It was September 13, 2001, just two days after the day that forever changed our country. It was just fifty-four hours after the moment that forever changed us all.

I felt so thankful for that initial phone call more than a year earlier.

"Lord, have mercy. Lord, have mercy."

God may be lurking behind that door, inside that call.

ADDITIONAL SCRIPTURES TO PONDER ON EMBRACING INTERRUPTIONS

[Abraham] looked up and noticed three men standing nearby. When he saw them, he ran to meet them and welcomed them, bowing low to the ground. . . . So Abraham ran back to the tent and said to Sarah, "Hurry! Get three large measures of your best flour, knead it into dough, and bake some bread." Then Abraham ran out to the herd and chose a tender calf and gave it to his servant, who quickly prepared it. (Gen 18:2, 6, 7)

Then [Elijah] lay down and slept under the broom tree. But as he was sleeping, an angel touched him and told him, "Get up and eat!" (1 Kgs 19:5)

The Ultimate Interruptions

So you, too, must keep watch! For you don't know what day your Lord is coming. (Matt 24:42)

Then [the farmer] said, "I know! I'll tear down my barns and build bigger ones. Then I'll have room enough to store all my wheat and other goods. And I'll sit back and say to myself, 'My friend, you have enough stored away for years to come. Now take it easy! Eat, drink, and be merry!'" But God said to him, "You fool! You will die this very night." (Luke 12:18–20)

When everything is ready, I [Jesus] will come and get you, so that you will always be with me where I am. (John 14:3)

4

Host Whole People Groups

After this I saw a vast crowd, too great to count, from every nation and tribe and people and language, standing in front of the throne and before the Lamb.

—Revelation 7:9

PRACTICING LARGE-SCALE HOSPITALITY

Once upon a time, there was a funky church that felt called by God to act as a *birthing station* for newly arrived immigrant churches. New Life Fellowship leased one large room from a local business in the Allston neighborhood of Boston and rolled up its sleeves.

We installed a (supposedly) soundproof curtain to divide the space for simultaneous worship services. New Life Church was the perceived American, English-speaking church and thus identified as the host, providing administrative oversight and electing the earliest Sunday worship slot, 9:00 a.m. We set up our microphones, drums, and keyboard, and turned on the six-by-six-inch white noise machine to begin our service—swwwwwwwiiiiii-issssssssssshhhhhhhhhhh—while the African Pentecostal church rehearsed with their microphones, electric guitars, keyboard, and drums on the other side of the curtain. By 10:00, we were both in full swing and the windows reverberated with praise, prayer, and preaching in French, Swahili, and English. Nothing mattered but God and people.

After lunch the Haitians arrived, their women's heads adorned in lace kerchiefs, energy radiating from the pastor and his flock. When the building had been broken into a third time, Martin, a post-PhD student from Germany, created bars from pipes and installed them over the windows. By evening, the Spanish and Brazilian churches were rocking the roof, the mice temporarily traumatized into hiding, trash cans overflowing with rich exotic scraps from potlucks throughout the day.

We shared the restrooms with a business that occupied two-thirds of the building. The employees were from a country whose reputation I will protect by not identifying it. As these folks worked seven days a week, we would run into each other in the ladies' and men's rooms. For some reason never understood by us, they seemed to take great delight in trashing les toilettes. Paper mountains consumed corners and avalanched onto floors while, in the sinks, unnamed organisms sailed amid green fuzz.

The worship space was rather pleasant, with our four-dollar plastic lawn chairs—except during a downpour, when one-quarter of the room became a reservoir, or when the furnace overslept, or the plumbing yawned.

We learned from experience what mattered most: God + people. We cried and laughed and prayed and lived our way through eight years of Ivy League training in collaborative ministry, hosting nine ethnically distinct churches. We didn't just encourage people to practice hospitality by inviting new friends over for dinner; we invited whole people groups into our hilarious space to worship freely, without criticism or dominance.

In 1997, New Life found itself on the cusp of homelessness. After prayer and inquiry, we launched the process that would culminate in the legal consolidation of New Life Church and Brighton Avenue Baptist Church into, voilà, International Community Church—An American Baptist Church. We began worshipping together July 5, 1998. The Burmese church was already sharing space with Brighton Avenue Baptist, as was a Haitian church, the latter of which quickly left when we became too noisy. Sorry. We brought the then Deaf Bible Study in our pocket with us, and they too became an autonomous Deaf church on October 25, 1998, with their leader Pastor Lamonte Grant.

Shortly thereafter, we received phone calls and knocks on the door from other churches anxious to share worship space. We rather quickly welcomed the Korean church under Rev. Inn Chung's pastorship and the first Brazilian church. Later, we included Pastor Vladimir Vezikov in planting a Russian-speaking church, for which we had long prayed. Another Brazilian church joined us later on, bringing us to seven churches—a little packed, but happy.

Once, a few church leaders made an appointment to inquire about sharing space with us. In many ways it sounded ideal, with their needs for other-than-Sunday hours, in a language unspoken by our other collaborative groups, bringing their mirthful traditions. As we were concluding our negotiations, one of them mentioned casually,

"We don't see eye-to-eye with so-and-so pastor here."

I immediately closed my notebook and said,

"Until you reconcile with your brother, we have nothing more to discuss."

Many organizations joined our ranks over the years, some too tiny to be self-sustaining, others too healthy to remain in a shared space—including a counseling center, a sound production studio, seminary classes, more than one Bible school, neighborhood parenting groups, peace organizations, the Boston Faith and Justice Network, and more. We love hosting organizations with short-term needs, such as the United States Census Bureau training and assistance center, an Eastern Service Workers concert, a neighborhood fundraiser, and so on.

A couple of devout Christians at a time occupy one room, rent-free, in exchange for work, security, and hospiradicality. They are our "resident custodians," a role they fill humbly and gratefully, in contrast to their seminary professorships back home.

We all seem to thrive on one another's distinctives, relishing the cultural intersections and diversions.

We purport that this is supercalifragilistichospitalitociousness, Bible-style.

Alikenesses tip the scale.

ADDITIONAL SCRIPTURES TO PONDER ON RADICALLY HOSTING WHOLE PEOPLE GROUPS

> You must not mistreat or oppress foreigners in any way. Remember, you yourselves were once foreigners in the land of Egypt. (Exod 22:21)
>
> These cities are for the protection of Israelites, foreigners living among you, and traveling merchants. (Num 35:15)
>
> Then the LORD said to Elijah, "Go and live in the village of Zarephath, near the city of Sidon." (1 Kgs 17:8–9)
>
> The LORD protects the foreigners among us. (Ps 146:9)
>
> "You must love the LORD your God with all your heart, all your soul, all your strength, and all your mind." And, "Love your neighbor as yourself." (Luke 10:27)
>
> Jesus said, "Make disciples of all the nations." (Matt 28:18–20)

Jesus had to go through Samaria. (John 4:4)

As for Philip, an angel of the Lord said to him, "Go south down the desert road that runs from Jerusalem to Gaza." So he started out, and he met the treasurer of Ethiopia, a eunuch of great authority under Kandake, the queen of Ethiopia. The eunuch had gone to Jerusalem to worship, and he was now returning. Seated in his carriage, he was reading aloud from the book of the prophet Isaiah. (Acts 8:26–28)

Don't forget to show hospitality to strangers, for some who have done this have entertained angels without realizing it! (Heb 13:2)

5

Listen for God's Wisdom

Fear of the LORD is the foundation of true wisdom. All who obey his commandments will grow in wisdom.

—PSALM 111:10

KEY WORDS

We were visiting Disney World for the second time in five years, intent on creating lifelong memories for our son. We couldn't wait to arrive at our favorite spot, MGM Studios, where the man greeting visitors offered to take a family snapshot with our camera. He slipped the gray strap over his hand and "dropped" it . . . our photo-treasures dangling six inches from his wrist. Slick.

It takes *exertion mentalis* to shift gears from praying, digging deep, planning, writing, wrestling, to vacation bliss *tout de suite*. But I was trying as MGM beckoned irrepressibly. No wonder I stopped in my haste, literally, when the Holy Spirit spoke into my mind louder than the crowds swirling past, all within a microsecond:

"My people. My word."

I knew instantly that God was riveting in me his top priorities, and, indeed, these words have grounded me through a plethora of competing demands, pulling and pushing, for many a year.

When we began ICC, our dear older folks understandably found us newcomers noisy and unsettling. Change is hard under the best of circumstances. But have forty-plus people join your space, and that is, well, stretching. Often, there were *senior tantrums*. I decided early on that I was going to be respectful and never, not even once, speak to them in anger or sarcasm. God gave me another slogan that guided me through those early years: *listen, love, and lead*. By God's grace, I would listen to their angst while praying that God would fill me with love for them (Rom 5:5). I pictured my head as a teapot. I lifted off the cover and imagined God pouring his love into me. Then I would simply do what was needed, sometimes commiserating:

"I'm sorry that change is so difficult, but you know we have to do this, don't you?"

Another time, God gave me a mental picture. When I was the target of their grief-turned-anger, I would visualize them in a plexiglass phone booth. The person was safe, couldn't hurt me or themselves, and constituted a crowd of one where no one else could hear them. When they had exhausted themselves, they simply emerged from the booth unscathed and we would go on.

One Sunday morning about twenty minutes before church, I passed through the office. Jim, who now laughs with the angels, was sitting in his black-and-white checkered trousers, thick, wavy cotton-white hair combed neatly to the side, eating a plain cruller.

"Good morning, Jim."

"Who moved that file cabinet?!"

I had turned it from one direction to another to accommodate desks for pastors sharing space. I won't repeat the words, but a tirade of volcanic proportions erupted from this usually fun-loving, sweet, eighty-something-year-old gentleman. His eyes had fire in them, his face turned ruby red, and his demeanor tightened drastically. I would have run for my nail-armor and fifteenth-century shield, but my feet were anviled to the spot.

I gave him my full attention, scrambling to cram him inside the phone booth, as he raved wildly out of control. Surely maritimers on the high seas, some twenty-five miles east of our building, heard him and, from shock, fumbled their big catch. When he was through, he sat for a moment, panting hard like a greyhound who had just won a race. I continued staring at him, speechless, with my jaw on the floor, probably drooling.

Just then, Jim burst into tears.

"All this clutter around here reminds me of Carolyn [his wife]. She's been gone six years, and I still don't know what I'm going to do."

Oh Jim. Dear, dear Jim. So sorry. A heart so broken. An amalgam of grief, anger, and fear. Jim accepted my assistance a little bit more after that day, letting me take him to appointments and errands. He was beloved in the neighborhood for his years of service on the community development corporation's board. Years after the file cabinet incident, his ride dropped him off after a board meeting, and Jim walked to his building's entrance and into the arms of Jesus. Just like that. He and Carolyn are together now, with no clutter.

What does this have to do with radical hospitality? If our own congregants resent each other, how can they appreciate whole congregations radically different from themselves?

THE RUSSIANS ARE COMING

The founding pastor of the Russian-speaking church drove from Providence to Boston (fifty miles each way) every Sunday afternoon after his own service because he had heard God whisper, "Go and plant a church for the myriad Russian speakers up north."

At his very first interchurch council gathering, he introduced himself to the other pastors in our building by announcing, "Look out, the Russians are coming!"—a phrase spoken with trepid humor during the Cold War era, but heard as an answer to prayer in this new millennium. And come they did. Pastor Vladimir Vezikov would drive adept violinist-children to Boston, accomplished pianists, families, and friends, and together they would invite Russian Bostonians to their church. Their portion of the lawn sign, printed in Russian, often captured the attention of passersby.

A Russian grandma flagged me down one time for a ride, and before I could ascertain whether or not she was a gun-toting impostor, she jumped into my car and began lamenting her loneliness. In the several blocks we rode together, I told her I pastored the English-speaking host church with the Russian sign out front, and she nearly ricocheted off the dashboard! Ecstatically, she noted the time of worship and thought she could not sleep a moment until Sunday. Surely, God's wisdom had sparked Vladimir's nomadic decision.

But, alas, it's nigh impossible for a pastor, supporting his family as an expert professional painter, to plant a church long-distance. So Pastor Vladimir prayed for God's guidance. Should he keep the church going? How much longer? And then, God in his unmistakable wisdom pricked the heart of another fledgling pastor, recently graduated from seminary, freshly ordained. Aha—yes, he would move to Boston, not temporarily, but for the long haul. He and his wife would pray for a home to purchase and raise their family here.

And so, the younger man took the reins, allowing Vladimir to pastor at a gentler pace. He still preaches the Russian sermon (their church has two sermons every

Sunday) and drives the distance with a full van. But what a deep joy to have detected God's wisdom in waiting for his plan to unfold. It is like reading Jeremiah 29:11 unselfishly, on behalf of, in his case, the younger pastor:

> "For I know the plans I have for *him*," says the Lord. They are plans for good and not for disaster, to give *him* a future and a hope."

Now, Vladimir basks under the preaching of Reverend Jan Vezikov, his son.

> *Love begins with those right under your nose.*
> *If your nose is bent out of shape, get a nose job.*

ADDITIONAL SCRIPTURES TO PONDER ON LISTENING FOR GOD'S WISDOM

Teach us to realize the brevity of life, so that we may grow in wisdom. (Ps 90:12)

Joyful is the person who finds wisdom, the one who gains understanding. For wisdom is more profitable than silver, and her wages are better than gold. Wisdom is more precious than rubies; nothing you desire can compare with her. She offers you long life in her right hand. She will guide you down delightful paths; all her ways are satisfying. Wisdom is a tree of life to those who embrace her; happy are those who hold her tightly. (Prov 3:13–18)

Better to hear the quiet words of a wise person than the shouts of a foolish king. Better to have wisdom than weapons of war. (Eccl 9:17–18)

> The gatekeeper opens the gate for him, and the sheep recognize his voice and come to him. He calls his own sheep by name and leads them out. After he has gathered his own flock, he walks ahead of them, and they follow him because they know his voice. They won't follow a stranger; they will run from him because they don't know his voice. . . . I am the good shepherd; I know my own sheep, and they know me. . . . I have other sheep, too, that are not in this sheepfold. I must bring them also. They will listen to my voice, and there will be one flock with one shepherd. (John 10:3–5, 14, 16)

> If you need wisdom, ask our generous God, and he will give it to you. He will not rebuke you for asking. (Jas 1:5)

> If someone says, "I love God," but hates a Christian brother or sister, that person is a liar; for if we don't love people we can see, how can we love God, whom we cannot see? And he has given us this command: Those who love God must also love their Christian brothers and sisters. (1 John 4:20–21)

6

Say "Yes" as Often as Possible

A man with leprosy came and knelt in front of Jesus, begging to be healed. "If you are willing, you can heal me and make me clean," he said. Moved with compassion, Jesus reached out and touched him. "I am willing," he said. "Be healed!"

—MARK 1:40–41

WELCOMING THE FRIENDS OF MR. BUTCH

"I see tons of tattooed young people on your yard all the time . . . so I figured if your church has all these rock shows, maybe you'd be okay with having Mr. Butch's memorial service here."

A woman from the neighborhood association was making funeral arrangements for the out-of-town family, and realized it could be widely attended.

Mr. Butch was a gregarious, well-known unhoused man who had occupied the streets of Allston for some three decades. And, yes, he had kept Marty's Liquors in business . . . but far more, he had kept people inspired. Mr. Butch had unharried time for hundreds and hundreds of people, listening to their ups and downs, offering childrearing advice, relationship counseling, and friendship. Everyone knew Mr. Butch. So when he was killed riding his pride-and-joy red scooter, the community lost one of its iconic best friends.

He wasn't a member of our church; in fact, he had never even come to an event or worship service. He may or may not have known the Lord. We didn't know the family or the people planning his final arrangements. The minister who would co-officiate was of a theological persuasion completely opposite mine. But saying no was unthinkable. Of course we would hold his funeral, with open hearts.

That July afternoon, the thermometer reached the 90s, so we had ICCers ready with plenty of water and fans turned on full blast. The New Orleans–style procession began with great dignity about three-quarters of a mile away, with us two ministers and Mr. Butch's sister and family following behind the band. We stopped at the site of his demise to lay a wreath and to hear his sister speak. In another ten minutes, the crowd overflowed the church, so much so that many stayed outside, listening through the windows.

There were shouts of commendation, buckets of tears, testimonials of his guidance, singing, praying, and, of course, a memorial service. I asked,

"How many of you consider yourselves Christians?"

About half or more signified, "Yeah!" and I proceeded to preach about access to heaven through Jesus the Christ. It was a sad, sacred day, culminating in deep conversations with his family and friends.

Some of Mr. Butch's ashes rest under our lawn sign. People still visit our church from time to time saying, "I was at Mr. Butch's funeral."

What if we had not said yes?

LAST-MINUTE WEDDING

Another time, a woman called sounding rather distraught. "I realize this is kind of last minute, but my fiancé and I want to get married in three weeks, over Thanksgiving, because our families will be here. We lived together a long time until we understood that it was godlier to be married first. So we are living separately now, and want more than anything to do things right!"

"What date are you considering?"

"The Saturday after Thanksgiving."

"Oh, wow . . . we have a major event scheduled for that evening, and we'll be setting up all day . . ."

"Oh." Her voice fell.

"... but come on over and let's talk."

The next day, she and her fiancé came by to see the building and chat. As I probed a bit more, I discovered that they were members of another wonderful church.

"So why don't you get married there?"

Reluctantly, she told me, "Well, we can't afford it. Our church charges $350 to use the sanctuary and another $300 for the pastor. We don't have enough money."

"So who will perform the wedding?"

"Our friend who is a reverend."

"Hmmmmm . . ." All well and good, but how can we do this logistically?

"Lord, can this work?"

As I pondered the schedule and prayed, again it felt right deep inside to say yes.

"What if you scheduled a late morning wedding with a small reception?"

And so they did. Their wedding was strikingly beautiful (of course) followed by a light lunch. Tragically, the women's purses, innocently left in a side room near the unlocked side door, were ransacked during the ceremony. But even desperate troublemakers only slightly clouded their glorious day. They were ever so happy, and our big Kee-lebration (for our friend Ralph Kee) went on the same day, a few hours later.

I see Mr. and Mrs. from time to time. And, yes, there is a special bond between them and our funky little church.

LET THE CHILDREN COME TO ME

Matt had been the initial booking agent and champion for the rock shows at ICC. He was tall, totally tattooed, charming, in his early thirties, married to a very bright, lovely woman, and daddy to a little girl and newborn son. When Caleb was about eighteen months old, Matt and his wife decided they wanted to have him baptized. So they began calling churches.

"No, I'm sorry. We can't help you until you take our classes and join the church. It will cost. . . ."

"Are you a member here? Your parents? Well then, I'm sorry."

Then Matt remembered, "The ICC. That's right too. They're a real church. Let me call."

"Yo, Matt. Okay. When can I come to your home?"

They lived outside the city, within walking distance to a little cove. Theirs was like a hobbit house, old, quaint New Englandish, with creaky floors and barn-board doors. As they told me how they met and all the achievements of their children, I dug deep into their spiritual lives and goals. I was horrified that here was a couple determined to take steps toward the living God and they could not find a church to accompany them! What is the church for? I felt outraged!

I explained Jesus to them, prayed with them, and planned their son's dedication around our conversations. It would be personal and holy. They brought about twenty friends and relatives that Sunday to witness this important moment for their nuclear family. We concluded their service with a few gifts and ICC's embrace. They invited a few of us to an elaborate feast at a downtown restaurant to celebrate this occasion which was strikingly sacred to them.

Do we see them in church? No. Did we plant and water seeds in lives cherished by God? Absolutely.

If you mean no, don't say yes.

ADDITIONAL SCRIPTURES TO PONDER ON SAYING YES HOSPIRADICALLY

Just say a simple, "Yes, I will," or "No, I won't." Anything beyond this is from the evil one. (Matt 5:37)

As surely as God is faithful, our word to you does not waver between "Yes" and "No." For Jesus Christ, the Son of God, does not waver between "Yes" and "No." He is the one whom Silas, Timothy, and I preached to you, and as God's ultimate "Yes," he always does what he says. For all of God's promises have been fulfilled in Christ with a resounding "Yes!" And through Christ, our "Amen" (which means "Yes") ascends to God for his glory. (2 Cor 1:18–20)

Cheerfully share your home with those who need a meal or a place to stay. (1 Pet 4:9)

7

Carpe Occasionem

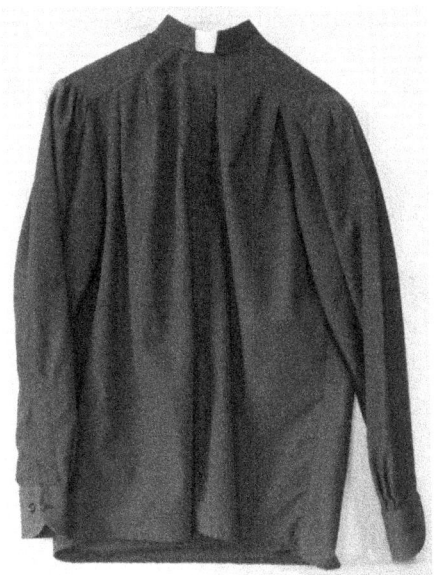

*Those too lazy to plow in the right season
will have no food at the harvest.*
—Proverbs 20:4

Never put off till tomorrow what you can do today.
—Thomas Jefferson

AN ORDINATION ENGINEERED BY THE HOLY SPIRIT

When he completed his Doctor of Ministry degree, Pastor Maung Maung Htwe's student visa expired, and, although his religious worker visa *should* have arrived in the mail by July, it hadn't. A man of exemplary integrity, Maung had always proceeded with impeccable legality throughout his eight years in the United States. Thus, he felt compelled to fly home to his wife and disabled daughter, whom he had never seen, with the hope of returning *une famille complète* just as soon as his R-1 came through.

Teresa, nicknamed Pearl, was born with severe developmental delay. Maung's wife Khin Khin Aye had worked with her tirelessly, trying to get her to stand, respond to verbal commands, even chew, all to little avail. It would be imperative for Pearl to receive advanced medical assessment and care first, then educational services second, all as soon as possible. But how? Where?

Maung was the second pastor of Overseas Burmese Christian Fellowship and had been a professor and then president of the Pwo Karen Theological Seminary in Yangon before coming to Boston for further education. He is a jovial, rotund man in his early thirties, dearly loved and respected by his congregants, students, and friends both back home and here in the States. If you can't find Saya Maung Maung Htwe, check the kitchen—he's probably coddling his infamous fish soup, which, second only to their societas with fellow countrymen, Buddhist Burmese refugees find so mesmerizingly alluring that they momentarily suppose themselves Christians while slurping.

Carpe Occasionem 43

Some five years earlier, Maung Maung Htwe had offered to be our test resident-custodian when we started ICC.

"I don't know anything about cleaning, Lorraine, but if you show me what to do, I'll do my best." He meant both parts of that statement.

One Sunday morning, when my husband and I arrived, the floors and furniture were garbed in sawdust from work completed the previous day. We found Maung on the brink of tears, broom in hand, sweeping futilely.

"No matter what I do, it doesn't get better!" Humble, teachable Maung, a genuine friend, a godly colleague, a man of God who knew how to live out Jesus' words, "Love each other in the same way I have loved you" (John 15:12).

And so, I had set aside the day before his departure from Boston. With a military salute, I announced, "Maung, I'm at your service. How can I help with packing or errands or whatever?"

"No, no, it's okay. I'm already packed." Then he sighed heavily,

"You know, there's only one thing I regret. I really, really wish I had been able to complete my ordination, because although I have two master's degrees, and a doctor of ministry, when I arrive home with no ordination, the people won't take me seriously as a real minister or real professor of theology."

I thought for a few seconds.

"So let's do it tonight!"

"Really?"

"Why not? You've been pastoring for several years now. You're right at the end of the ordination process, so it can be a bona fide local ordination. Then, when God clears the way for you to return to the States with your family, the American Baptists will simply recognize it, I'm sure. Come on . . . I'll call the officials and our church. You call your folks, and let's meet back here at seven."

So, our two churches gathered that evening to hear his ordination paper and give him a proper grilling. After a rousing council, his church voted unanimously to proceed. Then, right there on the spot, people volunteered to lead the various components of his ordination service—right down to the vows, a charge to the congregation, congregational music, special music, a prayer of ordination with the laying on of hands, presentation of an official ordination certificate, and even the gift of a black clergy shirt, purchased a few hours earlier. People buzzed in twos and threes. One seventy-something-year-old woman named Daisy whispered to me,

"I've never spoken in front of the church in my whole life. This will be the first time tonight!"

"Congratulations! You will be stellar. Just do it for Jesus and for Maung."

Half an hour later, we reassembled to conduct his ordination ceremony. The presence of the Holy Spirit in the room that night was palpable. We were all standing on holy ground, and not one of us doubted we were doing one of the most carpe occasionem-est things we had ever done. Niagaras of tears; sadness and joy.

Seven hours later, the now Reverend Dr. Maung Maung Htwe boarded a 747 for Burma, confident that he would be received and perceived as one anointed of God, worthy to address his own people with, in their minds, "proper" pastoral authority. Yes, people would follow his leadership now. Thy will be done.

Six weeks hence, the military junta massacred pro-democracy Buddhist monks and civilians. One academic year later, Cyclone Nargis assailed the Delta, as any and all Reverends, newly ordained or well-seasoned, found "parishioners" on every corner, at every wayside.

GRACE IN IMMIGRATION

Between his Boston-to-Burma and Burma-to-Boston travels, Maung had filed visa applications for his wife and two children twice, both rejected, once without even being reviewed. He intended to be a good father and husband and simply would not live away from them much longer, no matter the consequences. If they were denied visas again, he would go home to stay.

Always he asked for prayer. Pray for the visa process which was harrowing, expensive, intimidating, and upon which hinged his family's very lives. The final application was, however, approved. Miraculous! Thank God forever! Maung made plans to fly back to Boston, secure an apartment, then return home to escort his wife, disabled daughter, and infant son to the United States. The trip would be far too difficult for Khin Khin Aye alone.

When they arrived in Boston, I was stunned to discover just how disabled little Pearl actually was. Many tests later, doctors discovered numerous physical anomalies that they began to address, one of the most dramatic being a spasmodic intestine. Pearl regularly doubled over in her stroller in apparent pain, nonverbally crying out. She's had several operations already, including open-heart surgery, and faces several more. But, as physicians began repairing her body, she began to eat and grow and laugh and exude little pearls of hope around her.

The pure love and care afforded by her parents has been nothing shy of divine. They laugh and feed and carry and wash and cuddle her, and her younger brother kisses and plays around her. On Good Friday, Maung arrived with Pearl in his arms. She was amused and Maung laughed,

"Pearl is so happy because she knows in three days Jesus will rise from the dead!"

What if Maung Maung Htwe had not seized the moment in applying for their visas one last time?

> *The present does not exist;*
> *for in the moment of noticing, it evaporates.*

ADDITIONAL SCRIPTURES TO PONDER ON SEIZING THE MOMENT

But Moses told the people, "Don't be afraid. Just stand still and watch the Lord rescue you today." (Exod 14:13)

He is our God. We are the people he watches over, the flock under his care. If only you would listen to his voice today! (Ps 95:7)

That evening the disciples came to him and said, "This is a remote place, and it's already getting late. Send the crowds away so they can go to the villages and buy food for themselves." But Jesus said, "That isn't necessary—you feed them." (Matt 14:15–16)

Indeed, the "right time" is now. Today is the day of salvation. (2 Cor 6:2)

We must quickly carry out the tasks assigned us by the one who sent us. The night is coming, and then no one can work. (Heb 3:13)

8

Count the Cost Gladly

*If you want to be my disciple, you must hate everyone else
by comparison—your father and mother, wife and children,
brothers and sisters—yes, even your own life. Otherwise,
you cannot be my disciple. And if you do not carry
your own cross and follow me, you cannot be my disciple.
But don't begin until you count the cost.*

—Luke 14:26–28

COLANDER SLOGANS
DRAIN OFF THE EXCESS

- "The building supports ministry; not the other way around."
- "God first. Then . . . people before property, programs, paper, and protocol."
- "If something breaks, fix it, replace it, or throw it out."
- "The church is not a club, a business, a museum, or Grandma's house. It is a gathering place for people to connect with the living God."
- "If it's valuable and yours, take it home. If it's an antique that belongs to the church, we'll use it or sell it."
- "Things in common space are used in common."
- "I will live an unoffended life." —Mrs. F., New York City
- "Be confident, not cocky; gentle, not jelly; pious, not pompous; silly, not sarcastic."
- "Fight for your people, not with them."
- "Work hard on yourself, then put your own needs in your purse and concentrate on them."
- "Every Christian should have a spiritual director." — Pope Benedict XVI
- "Get people involved with people, and they'll care less about things."
- "Keep pointing people to Jesus."

- "Respect the past, but don't stay there."
- "This too shall pass!"
- "Let Scripture change you—not fear, not nostalgia."
- "Don't rush ahead of grace."
- "God is never flustered."
- "Listen, love, and lead."
- "My people, my word."
- "Differentiate."
- "Lean into it."

LOVING WILLIAM MORE THAN FURNITURE

One pastor leading his island-nation church in our shared building at New Life Fellowship had a sweet, affectionate son named William. As a youngster, he managed better when we assigned one adult to him during After-Supper Bible Camp and other combined children's gatherings. He never meant to break anything, it just sort of happened—within seconds. He was an enigma and left us in a quandary.

"How can we include him?"

We loved William, but braced ourselves when he arrived. His parents, realizing something was unique about him, exercised patience and protection, and, thankfully, were never unduly harsh, as far as we could notice.

We knew when their church had gathered the night before because the drum heads or a doorknob or table legs would require reassembling. Once, in thirty seconds flat, an entire skein of yarn was intricately wrapped around table and chair legs like the monster spider's web in Lord of the Rings. How could any human maneuver that prodigally?

As William turned ten, then eleven, he seemed more aware of people's reactions to his inability for self-control. Once, he sobbed softly in Judy's arms while she prayed with him:

"I don't mean to do it. I just can't help it."

Eventually, William was diagnosed and treated for Attention Deficit Hyperactivity Disorder and gradually began calming down. We lost touch with him, but recently learned that not only has he graduated from a prestigious exam high school in Boston, but also has earned his Bachelor of Science degree!

Lo those many years ago, whatever William may have broken pales in comparison to how we could have broken him had we not hung tough, by God's grace, counting the cost gladly.

Stuff is replaceable. Kids definitely are not.

WHEN THE DEAF CONGREGATION CRANKS IT UP

Immanuel Deaf Church used to worship in the large auditorium while we occupied the sanctuary. It began to feel too expansive for them, as did the sanctuary when they were there for special occasions, so, after several years, they asked to relocate to a midsized room in the basement. I felt uncomfortable having any church worship *down below*, but they insisted. They scrubbed and waxed the floor and walls, hung banners, drew pictures on the white board, and generally transformed the space into a most welcoming environ.

Other churches worship above them now in the same cavernous auditorium. Sometimes it's our church, sometimes another. Just as our music concludes and we enter the more pensive segment of sermon with special prayer, Immanuel Deaf Church launches into their music. The keyboard is programmed with a repetitious refrain and Izzy cranks it up for both bone and wood conduction, appealing to the profoundly Deaf and the Hard of Hearing. I notice visitors glancing around, wondering where the disturbance originates. But regular ICCers rarely flinch; rather, a smile or two creeps across faces. If I think of it I might comment:

"And as our Deaf friends continue their passionate worship, let's pray together."

Or, "Of all the churches here, the Deaf church is the loudest." And people chuckle.

Is this part of counting the cost gladly? The greater cost would be tabulated as loss were they not among us.

Our two churches were letting out at about the same time, and our folks were intermingling—always a thrilling, holy wonder. The kids from our church and the Deaf church were playing and giggling near some grownups who were exchanging demographic backgrounds.

"I'm from Jamaica and Boston. You?"

"I'm from DR [Dominican Republic] and RI [Rhode Island]," signed the other.

One of the kids jumped in, "I'm from Alaska."

Then, with emphatic confidence, a Hearing child of Deaf parents declared, "I'm African American and Deaf."

And, yes, she is.

We thank You, O Holy Trinity,
that you are God and we are not.[1]

ADDITIONAL SCRIPTURES TO PONDER ON GLADLY COUNTING THE COST

Yes, everything else is worthless when compared with the infinite value of knowing Christ Jesus my Lord. For his sake I have discarded everything else, counting it all as garbage, so that I could gain Christ. . . . I want to know Christ and experience the mighty power that raised him from the dead. I want to suffer with him, sharing in his death. (Phil 3:8, 10)

Because of the joy awaiting him, he endured the cross, disregarding its shame. Now he is seated in the place of honor beside God's throne. Think of all the hostility he endured from sinful people; then you won't become weary and give up. (Heb 12:2–3)

---

1. Prayer heard at Schloss Mittersill International Christian Conference and Study Centre, A-5730, Mittersill, Austria, 2006.

Dear brothers and sisters, when troubles come your way, consider it an opportunity for great joy. For you know that when your faith is tested, your endurance has a chance to grow. So let it grow, for when your endurance is fully developed, you will be perfect and complete, needing nothing. (Jas 1:2–4)

Though you do not see him now, you trust him; and you rejoice with a glorious, inexpressible joy. (1 Pet 1:8)

Remember, it is better to suffer for doing good, if that is what God wants, than to suffer for doing wrong! (1 Pet 3:17)

You have patiently suffered for me without quitting. But I have this complaint against you. You don't love me or each other as you did at first! Look how far you have fallen! (Rev 2:3–5)

9

Keep the Infrastructure as Self-Managing as Possible

SIMPLE GIFTS[1]

'Tis the gift to be simple, 'tis the gift to be free.
'Tis the gift to come down where we ought to be.
And when we find ourselves in the place just right,
'Twill be in the valley of love and delight.
When true simplicity is gain'd,
To bow and bend we shan't be asham'd,
To turn, turn will be our delight,
Till by turning, turning we come 'round right.

1. *Simple Gifts*, Elder Joseph Brackett, Shaker Community, Alfred, Maine, 1848.

THE NUTS AND BOLTS OF SCHEDULING

ICC leaders meet with each church, group, and resident-custodian annually to review and renegotiate their covenants. In addition, I meet with the pastors and leaders six to eight times a year in what we call the interchurch council. They're good times, usually like a mini-retreat. Immediately after opening devotions, we set the date of our next council. Then, we go around the room updating each other on recent God-sightings within our church or group, reporting where we have seen God at work. Next, we discuss plans for any upcoming collaborative worship, feast, event, or celebration. Lastly, we discuss property issues, which by this time have slid into their proper niche of being far less urgent than the needs of people. We end in prayer offered in various languages.

We have shared much over the years, being vulnerable, creating empathy, praying for each other's flocks and families, solving problems, making decisions. It has been out of these hours of trust and disclosure, discussion and prayer, that we have urged our churches to embrace one another too.

Still, back in the early days, we lacked a tool to keep us organized. And since there was never enough income to hire an administrator or secretary, we needed an infrastructure that was as simple and self-managing as possible. I saw a huge magnetic calendar in the faculty lounge of a Christian school and thought, "That's it. But how should we structure it?"

In walks Jean Ehsay.

Jean was a woman of prayer and faith who exuded the joy of the Lord, right to the end of her battle with cancer.

She had needed to stop working, but was never ready to cease serving her Lord. Continually, she exhorted her husband, Henry; son, Bright; her church, Overseas Burmese Christian Fellowship; me; and others to give their all to God, and she practiced what she preached. One day, she asked,

"Lorraine, is there anything I can do from home to help you?"

"Yes! Would you help me think through how we can design a workable system with this magnetic master calendar?"

I brought the whole big board with dozens of colored magnets to her home where we laid it out on her living room floor and brainstormed. Jean sat on her couch resting, her hairless head wrapped in a scarf, and I crawled around the floor turning magnets and lines this way and that. On that brown carpet was midwifed the idea of identifying churches and groups by color and having them sign up for rooms quarterly. Her pastor drafted the building's layout so people could reserve space by writing on their magnet a room's initials and hours required. Brilliant! After all, *it's all in the calendar*. First come, first served, with several exceptions: funerals, then weddings, preempt all. And Friday evening through Saturday evening is designated "flex" space in deference to special celebrations and events. It works with remarkable alacrity!

Toward the end, Jean grew very thin and kept her balding head warm with kerchiefs and hats. The founding pastor of her church, Rev. Zaw Wynn Tan, visited her regularly, of course, as he had grown up around her back home. Their families were close. When the time came, Zaw Wynn preached at her funeral—a difficult, holy affair.

Several months later, we held our annual collaborative Good Friday service, for which he had randomly been assigned, "Woman, behold your son. Behold your mother." He decided to share Jean's words to him the last time he visited with her. She had weakly exhorted him,

"Zaw Wynn, take care of the church."

His Good Friday sermonette was poignant: Jesus entrusted his mother to his closest friend, John, and Jean Ehsay, as a mother of the church, entrusted her family in Christ to her son in the faith. Rivers of tears.

Thank you, God, for Jean, whose legacy lives on and enables us to host whole people groups with surprisingly little conflict. These days, Jean helps the angels keep heaven well organized!

Use what you've got and who you've got.[2]

ADDITIONAL SCRIPTURES TO PONDER ON SIMPLE, SELF-MANAGING INFRASTRUCTURE

True wisdom is not a simple matter. (Job 11:6)

Pay careful attention to your own work, for then you will get the satisfaction of a job well done, and you won't need to compare yourself to anyone else. For we are each responsible for our own conduct. (Gal 6:4–5)

We never accepted food from anyone without paying for it. We worked hard day and night so we would not be a burden to any of you. (2 Thess 3:8)

---

2. A favorite saying of my dear friend Judy Kee.

10

Drop Negative Signs and Business Lingo

*May the words of my mouth
and the meditation of my heart
be pleasing to you,
O L<small>ORD</small>, my rock and my redeemer.*

—P<small>SALM</small> 19:14

CHANGING NEGATIVES TO POSITIVES

I never saw such dollhouse-sized padlocks!

"What's in here?"

"Dishes."

Nearly every cupboard and closet was locked. One of the many initial tasks was to gently remove the locks, while *listening, loving, and leading*, until only offices, residences, and church-specific storage cabinets were locked.

Signs had to be adjusted from *Don't Touch!* to *You may touch the air around the statue* (admittedly that one was over the top), from *Stay Out!* to *Please Select Another Room Tonight*, from *Stay Off the Grass* to *Thank You for Not Driving across Grass*, from *Keep Out!* to *Private*, from *Be Quiet* to *Concert in Progress*, and more.

We try to tell people what *to* do, not what *not* to do. The educational curve was, and, at times, still is, steep. But it's wonderful for folks to feel wanted in a room, not *not* wanted.

ALONGSIDE IS BETTER THAN OVER

For several years, Lamonte had been the last and sole student at Deaf Immanuel Bible Institute, an offshoot of Theological Education of the Deaf at CUME (the Center for Urban Ministerial Education), Gordon-Conwell Theological Seminary's Boston campus. TED, as it was endearingly known, ran for five all-too-short years before the seminary closed it in a period of fiscal panic. Though I was devastated, six months later, I decided to continue it as a church-based learning center for Deaf pastors in training.

Tall, lanky Lamonte, with a smile as wide as the Congo and a heart as wise as a migrating butterfly, inhaled theological education like a pallid seagull stranded in the Serengeti. He had been called—no, captured—by the Deaf community to be their pastor and was learning all he could, wherever he could.

Before his children were born, Lamonte's energy seemed unmitigated. (Once kids enter the equation, no parent gets enough sleep for fifteen years.) His schedule was packed with evangelism, home visits, prayer gatherings, worship, retreats, and more. One of my favorites was his two-hour Thursday night Bible study.

Names, first and last, accurately finger-spelled, are important to the Deaf. So, this evening, a visitor introduced herself to the group, and Lamonte made sure that everyone in the semicircle did the same. After I introduced myself, however, Lamonte said,

"She is the Hearing pastor over me."

"Hold on ... *alongside* you," I signed. "Only *God* is over us; we minister together, brothers and sisters in Christ!"

"Right, right," he agreed. Then, he signed, "Mother. She's my mother. I'm her son!"

"That's a little better," I fancied to myself, "and actually, rather sweet."

BRING A SPIRIT OF WORSHIP TO THE BUSINESS OF THE CHURCH

Years ago, I was ruminating on the disparate incongruity between a worship service and a business meeting. In one room, people act and sing like angels; in the adjoining room an hour later, they become rabid attack dogs. Is it so difficult to apply the Scriptures that we cannot compromise on the shade of paint?

I remember long ago fasting solemnly before an annual business meeting, praying that we could complete the agenda without actual fights breaking out. We did. I was starved.

Perhaps it was the cumulative trauma of business meetings and their tedium that nudged me in an alternate direction. "Lord, how can we do this?" We began holding our annual meeting *during* the worship service and calling it our Annual Ministry Update Gathering. We had the clerk's report during the welcome, treasurer's during the offering, missions as the Missions Moment, and so on. My report was written as the sermon, after which we would celebrate communion. Then, for a couple of years, we framed the whole morning as exhibit tables with each ministry creating a display board to visualize their report rather than reading it. More recently, we've crafted an altar in the center of the room with each ministry team placing a representation of their written report. Then, people promise soulfully to read each report at home. Do they? Hmmm.

We continue to tweak the format and process of our Annual Ministry Update Gathering from year to year. We still need to hear people's ideas, concerns, dreams, and doubts, and hopefully can create that forum during weekly adult discussion time and home prayer visits.

But, admittedly, it's preferable and rather delightful to celebrate with a grateful heart than to fuss with grumpy complaints.

SPEAK THE LANGUAGE OF COLLABORATION

From ICC's inception, we dropped business lingo like creepy worms, because the vocabulary we use to describe our ethos affects both our atmosphere and our relationships. Hear yourself speaking new words:

From	"Tenant"	To	"Collaborator"
From	"Rent"	To	"Shared expenses"
From	"Contract"	To	"Covenant"
From	"But we've always . . ."	To	"Good idea!"
From	"We never did it that way before"	To	"Let's try it."
From	"Owned"	To	"Shared"
From	"No"	To	"Yes"
From	"Business Meeting"	To	"Ministry Update Gathering"
From	"Meeting"	To	"Brainstorming"
From	"Committee"	To	"Ministry Team"
From	"Mine"	To	"Ours"
From	"Our church's"	To	"Our churches'"
From	"Them"	To	"Us"
From	"Odors"	To	"Aromas"
From	"Church member"	To	"Friend"
From	"Dirty kitchen"	To	"Happy kitchen"
From	"Noisy"	To	"Passionate"
From	"What??"	To	"Could you reword that, please?"
From	silence	To	"Thank you"

... and more.

Respectful words transform demands into desires.
Address the heart, not just the head.

ADDITIONAL SCRIPTURES TO PONDER ON USING POSITIVE AND COVENANTAL LANGUAGE

A gentle answer deflects anger, but harsh words make tempers flare. The tongue of the wise makes knowledge appealing, but the mouth of a fool belches out foolishness. (Prov 15:1)

Kind words are like honey— sweet to the soul and healthy for the body. (Prov 16:24)

Better to be patient than powerful. (Prov 16:32)

Soft speech can break bones. (Prov 25:15)

A quiet spirit can overcome even great mistakes. (Eccl 10:4)

I no longer call you slaves. . . . Now you are my friends. (John 15:15)

Understand this, my dear brothers and sisters: You must all be quick to listen, slow to speak, and slow to get angry. Human anger does not produce the righteousness God desires. (Jas 1:19–20)

Don't grumble about each other, brothers and sisters. (Jas 5:9)

11

Have as Few Rules to Enforce as Possible

Jesus replied, "'You must love the L<small>ORD</small> your God with all your heart, all your soul, and all your mind.' This is the first and greatest commandment. A second is equally important: 'Love your neighbor as yourself.' The entire law and all the demands of the prophets are based on these two commandments."

—M<small>ATTHEW</small> 22:37–40

THREE BASIC RULES

How many rules can a person remember, let alone follow? So we've kept it real simple for ourselves and everyone we host.

In fact, this chapter models our simplicity. Three major rules:

1. *Love as Jesus Loves.* The first is admittedly the toughest, where our blind spots ferment.
2. *Violence-Free.* Anyone is welcome; violence of any kind is not.
3. *KWAAAT = Kids With Adults At All Times.* Our kids are our treasures; keeping them safe is priority number one.

Two minor rules, often challenged in public places: "GUM" and "SMOKING" with lines through them.

> *What matters most is what matters to God.*
> *(Gum and cigarettes most likely do not make*
> *God's list.)*

ADDITIONAL SCRIPTURES TO PONDER ON HOSTING WITH MINIMAL RULES

What sorrow awaits you teachers of religious law and you Pharisees. Hypocrites! For you are so careful to clean the outside of the cup and the dish, but inside you are filthy—full of greed and self-indulgence! (Matt 23:25–26)

> "Yes," said Jesus, "what sorrow also awaits you experts in religious law! For you crush people with unbearable religious demands, and you never lift a finger to ease the burden." (Luke 11:46)

> He has enabled us to be ministers of his new covenant. This is a covenant not of written laws, but of the Spirit. The old written covenant ends in death; but under the new covenant, the Spirit gives life. (2 Cor 3:6)

12

Set Grace-Plumped Boundaries and Leave the Maturing to God

Love is patient and kind. Love is not jealous or boastful or proud or rude. It does not demand its own way. It is not irritable, and it keeps no record of being wronged. It does not rejoice about injustice but rejoices whenever the truth wins out. Love never gives up, never loses faith, is always hopeful, and endures through every circumstance. Prophecy and speaking in unknown languages and special knowledge will become useless. But love will last forever!

—1 Corinthians 13:4–8

HOLD THE PHONE

Many years ago, friends of a church member had a son who was accepted to a college in Boston. Expenses for international students are astronomical, so you can imagine their relief when they discovered we could offer a free room for their son in exchange for property maintenance. Perfect. During our interview, Daniel presented himself as a careful Christian, accustomed to hard work, with a servant's heart. Perfect.

For several months, our newcomer ardently swept and mopped and carried out trash, until the glow of earning his keep by less-than-glamorous means waned. His gusto went on life support. Of course, comatose chores can go undiagnosed for weeks with a shot of tidying up or a dose of under-the-couch caching.

"After all, he's just barely twenty years old, still learning. Patience."

Months into his tenure, we received a preposterous phone bill which was obviously not church-related. When we traced the $1,000 debt to our angel-faced young man who had assertively exhausted himself with work, we inquired,

"By any chance, Daniel, have you made phone calls to (ahem) Taiwan, Norway, South Africa, Corsica, Belgium, Milan, French Riviera, Cancun, Tuscany, Santa Barbara, Oahu, Bali?"

Mind you, this was in the day when cell phones and the internet appeared only in sci-fi movies and long-distance telephoning required a six-figure salary. Well (ahem), he *may have* a vague recollection of placing one or two out-of-the-country calls, but for family emergencies only, naturally. Naturally. A month or so later, he appeared in my office looking ever so slightly contrite. I wasn't sure or not if I was detecting a teensy smirk inside those twinkling, baby-faced eyes as he said,

"I'll pay off that bill, even though my memory fails me. I appreciate being able to earn my room here, as I need to finish out the semester without the expense of on-campus housing."

Dementia at age twenty? Curiously, the phone number listed on the bill was identical to his—dozens of times.

"Just as I suspected, some masked intruder has picked the lock, sneaked into my room here, and used my phone. Blast!"

We waited. No check. More phone bills. We changed the phone service to permit only metro calls, blocking all others. Still no payment—not a dime. To top it off, when we invited visitors to alight on one of our couches, they would roll off the bulging seats before taking a peek underneath. We would have to leave his maturing to God (what better way). We had set generous boundaries, but, alas, we had to ask Daniel to leave before the semester ended.

I spotted him once after that and honked the horn. He smiled and waved demonstrably. His clothes were clean; he looked rested and well fed, and was apparently not living under a highway overpass. I'm told his mother was mortified and desperately wished to rectify his debt, but was completely helpless. Stiffing a church was never included in their family values.

I've read that the frontal lobe of the male brain, responsible for planning ahead and grasping behavioral consequences, does not reach full development until age twenty-one or twenty-two. The church budget couldn't wait for his cerebral cortex to mature. He was God's project.

COLLABORATION DEFICIT

Another time, a church had shared our building for several years. They were overseen by a group that regularly rotated leadership, so, at this point, the congregation was on their fourth pastor. They were absolutely delightful folks, polite, very godly. In fact, their prayer gatherings often spanned the night. Their music was heavenly, their preaching—though in a language unknown to me—seemed effectively riveting, their dinners were sumptuous, and our relationships were filial. They certainly contributed their shared expenses punctually and kept their covenant responsibly, except for one elephant-in-the-room omission: they refused to collaborate.

As time went along, the way in which they passively boycotted collaborative worship services, prayer gatherings, feasts, festivals, holiday celebrations including Holy Week events, and interchurch councils became unsettling. With smiles on their faces, their leaders would explain that they were holding their own dinner or worship or celebration separate from the rest of us. Of course, we encourage autonomy by not interfering with each other's churches, but we also expect groups to fellowship within the whole collaborative at least once a year and to send representatives to the interchurch council. As every other group had done, they, too, had signed the same covenantal agreement. Their passive resistance was pulling down overall morale, as consistently they could not, would not, join any combined gathering. We had set what we and others agreed were generous, grace-plumped boundaries, but, in the end, were constrained to replace their group with another church. How sad.

Certainly, we have learned that collaborating in ministry is not for every leader or for every church or group. In theory, it sounds scintillating, but, in reality, it can require jaw-clenching self-control, unnatural humility, deference, and other-centeredness versus me-centeredness. The power of the apology and the health of forgiveness must resound within our walls, because once again—drat—we all minister with underdeveloped cerebral cortexes.

Lord, thank you for your eternal patience with us. Give us silos of grace to minister alongside others, with your foresight in building not our own congregational kingdoms, but yours. Thank you for laying in our lap a fast-track opportunity to become a bit more Christlike and to be stretched in ways that most assuredly will at times sting. Teach us the *verbalis* of love, and enable us imperfect characters to point people to the perfect Creator of the universe. In the magnificent name of the Resurrected Jesus. Amen.

> *Justice is higher than unity,*
> *and love is higher than justice.*

ADDITIONAL SCRIPTURES TO PONDER ON SETTING GENEROUS BOUNDARIES AND LEAVING THE MATURING TO GOD

Oh, the joys of those who do not follow the advice of the wicked, or stand around with sinners, or join in with mockers. But they delight in the law of the Lord. (Ps 1:1)

If only you would listen to his voice today! The Lord says, "Don't harden your hearts." (Ps 95:7–8)

> Your own ears will hear him. Right behind you a voice will say, "This is the way you should go," whether to the right or to the left. (Isa 30:21)

> And so, dear brothers and sisters, I plead with you to give your bodies to God because of all he has done for you. Let them be a living and holy sacrifice—the kind he will find acceptable. This is truly the way to worship him. Don't copy the behavior and customs of this world, but let God transform you into a new person by changing the way you think. Then you will learn to know God's will for you, which is good and pleasing and perfect. Because of the privilege and authority God has given me, I give each of you this warning: Don't think you are better than you really are. Be honest in your evaluation of yourselves, measuring yourselves by the faith God has given us. (Rom 12:1–3)

> Again I say, don't get involved in foolish, ignorant arguments that only start fights. A servant of the Lord must not quarrel but must be kind to everyone, be able to teach, and be patient with difficult people. (2 Tim 2:23–24)

> Therefore, since we are surrounded by such a huge crowd of witnesses to the life of faith, let us strip off every weight that slows us down, especially the sin that so easily trips us up. And let us run with endurance the race God has set before us. We do this by keeping our eyes on Jesus, the champion who initiates and perfects our faith. (Heb 12:1–3)

13

Take Prayerful Risks

When you see the Levitical priests carrying the Ark of the Covenant of the LORD your God, move out from your positions and follow them. Since you have never traveled this way before. . . . Then Joshua told the people, "Purify yourselves, for tomorrow the LORD will do great wonders among you."

—JOSHUA 3:3–5

*This is my command—be strong and courageous!
Do not be afraid or discouraged. For the L*ORD *your
God is with you wherever you go."*

—Joshua 1:9

HARDCORE FAITH

"Hello? International Community Chur-rch."

"Hello. My name is Eric. I'm trying to find a church where I can hold some concerts for youth, and every one I've tried has said no. Since I live in the neighborhood, I thought I'd give you a call."

"Hello, Eric. I'm the pastor here. What kind of concerts do you have in mind?" I'm thinking flutes and plastic recorders.

"Hardcore rock concerts. I want a church where kids can listen to their favorite bands in a safe, positive environment. We were doing this in another church for awhile, but they couldn't continue, so I'm checking around."

"Mm-HMM-mm," I croaked. "Well. Why don't you come over so we can meet each other and talk. When can you come?"

So, that fall day, a well-mannered, reserved, yet gregarious twenty-two-year-old, dressed in jeans, black band-logoed sweatshirt, and army cap, sat across the table and poured out his passion for impacting young people, not with the gospel, but with, as he put it, *positive music.*

"I want to impact *him* with the gospel."

Take Prayerful Risks 75

This was the first of thousands of conversations, spanning at least ten gazillion hours of planning, negotiating, briefing, debriefing, guiding, praying, and my learning about a culture I had never experienced.

Prayerful risks?

Since the first show was on our son's seventeenth birthday, which we were having with the youth group, the date is sealed in my memory. About fifty kids showed up (for the concert, not the party)—a disappointment for Eric. The volume was understatedly deafening. Our church kids were intimidated by the whole scene and preferred to hunker down in the basement for ping-pong and birthday cake.

Over the next two years, as I attended hardcore show after hardcore show, I freaked out less and less.

"Eric, what are they singing? Can you understand the lyrics? What are those kids doing over there . . . they're flailing their arms . . . I think a fight's breaking out!" No way. They were slam dancing with actual rhythmic steps.

Gradually, I relaxed in my role as Pastor of the Show, a hat I eagerly shared with other pastor-types as much for their sakes as mine. These kids were not what churches thought. They were young people with hearts and minds like any others . . . just hiding behind tattoos and costumed outfits, piercings and dos. I came to know scores of them, though still excavating my brain for their names, and hundreds more by face.

Eric enlisted his own crew, oriented them to the building and to their responsibilities, and made sure they remained vigilant. A few church kids and young adults helped out for a season now and then, but mostly Eric found unchurched kids. He and they worked their toenails off. They arrived four or five hours early to move heavy oak chairs and non-folding tables with pipe legs, cordon off hallways and rooms, arrange the sound system and lighting, and pamper the big-shot musicians—which, seriously, many of them were.

I wore a snazzy nametag and stuffed wads of paper towel in my ears, until I caught onto those yellow foam earplugs. My role was to prayer-walk throughout the shows, making sure the kids, musicians, their crews, our crew, parents, and Eric remained at the Throne. I introduced myself to people and silently asked God for at least one substantial conversation during each show. Usually, there were several. During one particular prayer-stroll outside, I bumped into a woman who had driven her teenage daughter and friends to the show. She had Lou Gehrig's Disease and communicated via a small white board. She was a Christian, doing her part in reaching hardcore kids for Christ, supporting their *positive music*, especially Christian hardcore. Her name was Cathy, but to all the kids, she was Punk Rock Mom. What an inspiration!

Though I began to droop by ten o'clock, Eric and his crew remained until every last empty water bottle was thrown out, bathrooms were scrubbed, heavy furniture replaced for Sunday morning, and lights were off—around midnight. It would be impossible for the angels to clean every scridgen of dirt after hundreds of kids had generated a ninety-five-degree hardcore greenhouse, with condensation raining down the walls and turning furniture to glue. Conscientious as he was after working bitterly hard for ten or so hours, the joke became, "Someone's always mad at

Eric." The next day, that one rogue water bottle would flaunt itself at the feet of whoever was having a bad day.

Money. Hundreds of *suggested donations* must be fattening the coffers of the church, or maybe the coordinator? This time, the joke was on everyone else. Remuneration for musicians, especially when they were famous, more often than not required Eric to withdraw his own money from the automatic teller machine to compensate for less-than-adequate revenue.

Yes indeed, I would fight for this vanguard ministry.

I called this raw pre-evangelism and seed planting. Of course, Eric has always been the linchpin. I felt the Holy Spirit had whispered to me, "Invest in this guy," and so I did.

Two years into the shows, Eric joined our Alpha program. It was during the Holy Spirit weekend retreat that he gave his life to the Resurrected Jesus and determined to live for him the best he could, by God's grace. Oceans of tears. Months later, during Palm Sunday weekend, we would witness one of the most memorable times ever. Saturday, the Solid State Tour did The ICC, as the kids affectionately named us. They were five record-labeled Christian bands doing a hardcore show at our little venue of a church auditorium. The show sold out to 420 standing, screaming young people. Afterward, the sweat-sopped musicians hung around to talk to the concertgoers. They explained the gospel, shared their personal stories of redemption, prayed with kids, and left the mark of the King of Kings on hundreds of hearts.

The next morning, I baptized Eric. It was Palm Sunday, the three-year memorial of his father's death. Eric stood before the congregation and told how he had given his heart to Christ and what being baptized meant to him. We both described the indescribable previous evening and were overcome with emotive gratitude to God. I always let baptismal candidates select someone to assist me in the water, and Eric had chosen his younger brother, who had staffed the stage for last night's show. Everyone seemed to be on their extra-best behavior when they saw him staring at them, for Andy is literally covered in tattoos, including his shaved head and fingers, a detail that has nothing to do with anything—except its ability to elicit bulging eyes. Andy remains on the edge of becoming a Christian, a seed straining toward the sun. Eric's baptism right after the Solid State Tour ranks right up there for me with an intergalactic vacation.

Yes, I admit that on occasion I have asked God, "Tell me again, Lord, why are we doing these shows?"

At least five times, I've been one inch away from pulling the plug. Then, I feel God's hand on my soul-shoulder saying, "Wait." So, I've continued to fight for Eric, fight for the shows, fight for these misunderstood kids, and fight for the seeds planted. I, for one, am a more compassionate Christian because of them.

One of our former residents reminds me of the hardcore show when, outside his door, he heard a scuffle between two guys. He grabbed his baseball bat to come to my rescue. (What in the world?) When he opened his door, he saw me looking up into the face of a tall, tough, burly guy, calming him down. And he was looking down into my eyes, nodding ruefully.

"Okay, I will. Sorry. I promise."

I don't recall it.

The fire department knows us. The nearby hospital. The ambulance service. Certainly the neighbors. The city councilor. The police like us the best, because, as they tell us, we make their job easier for one evening. They've been exceedingly supportive, and for that we remain very grateful.

Over the decade of rock shows, we estimate conservatively that twenty thousand young people have attended concerts. We continue praying that God will water and aerate the seeds planted, fighting back anything that would choke their fragile growth, until one day many will find Jesus to be all that we have striven to show him to be. "Lord may many of these dear younger people invite you to be their best Friend and Savior as they realize you are for them, not against them. Amen."

What if I *had* pulled the plug six years ago, weary of the risk? Thank God for his restraint.

If you're going to take a risk, make it big![1]

ADDITIONAL SCRIPTURES TO PONDER ON TAKING PRAYERFUL RISKS

Trust in the LORD with all your heart; do not depend on your own understanding. Seek his will in all you do, and he will show you which path to take. Don't be impressed with your own wisdom. Instead, fear the LORD and turn away from evil. (Prov 3:5–7)

---

1. Rev. Ralph Kee.

> As the time drew near for him to ascend to heaven, Jesus resolutely set out for Jerusalem. (Luke 9:51)
>
> Jesus fully realized all that was going to happen to him, so he stepped forward to meet them. "Who are you looking for?" he asked. "Jesus the Nazarene," they replied. "I Am he," Jesus said. (Judas, who betrayed him, was standing with them.) As Jesus said "I Am he," they all drew back and fell to the ground! Once more he asked them, "Who are you looking for?" And again they replied, "Jesus the Nazarene." "I told you that I Am he," Jesus said. "And since I am the one you want, let these others go." He did this to fulfill his own statement: "I did not lose a single one of those you have given me." Then Simon Peter drew a sword and slashed off the right ear of Malchus, the high priest's slave. But Jesus said to Peter, "Put your sword back into its sheath. Shall I not drink from the cup of suffering the Father has given me?" (John 18:4–11)
>
> And now I [Paul] am bound by the Spirit to go to Jerusalem. I don't know what awaits me. (Acts 20:22)

14

Celebrate Cultural and Linguistic Distinctives

At the name of Jesus every knee should bow, in heaven and on earth and under the earth, and every tongue confess that Jesus Christ is Lord, to the glory of God the Father.

—PHILIPPIANS 2:10–11

A CORNUCOPIA OF WORSHIP

What a treat to worship with each of our collaborating churches!

The Deaf church plays electronically programmed music that is loud with a capital L, and repetitious. The sound is conducted through wood and bones, enriching their worship experience. Some Deaf are actually hard-of-hearing or have minimal hearing, making music and percussion particularly rich. Their Hearing children fit right in, generally until they crave the company of other Hearing young people. The Deaf miss some information on fliers, calendars, posters, and emails because American Sign Language (or, some other national sign language such as Russian or Portuguese or French Sign) is their native language, not written English. Theirs is a language that cannot be written, is visual not literary, and touches us all, especially during their demonstrative dramas that communicate fairly well even without an interpreter.

The Korean church begins their worship in silence, we at ICC in gregariousness. Their music is rich and robust, Christian and cultural; ours hymnodical and contemporary. When I asked Rev. Lee how they ministered to their young people, he said, "We keep them in a chamber"—a chamber orchestra, that is! Each Korean teen plays an instrument in the orchestra that accompanies worship every Sunday. And then their gracious hospitality is like that of the Burmese church: quantities of succulent food accompanied by an open invitation. Ours is a monthly potluck dinner and weekly refreshments. Marge grew up in this church building, and turning ninety years old does not deter her from rising early enough to bake us a cake each Sunday. You're the best, Marge.

The Russian church stands up during Scripture readings and conducts a highly structured, meticulously pointed worship flow, while the Burmese church involves their children and teens in liturgy and never bats an eye when little tots run up and down the aisle. The children never disturb equipment and are carried out if they cry. They obviously feel at home in their church. Furthermore, the Burmese church cooks every Sunday, their exotic, savory aromas permeating the building. The Russian church enjoys a quieter service, similar to the Koreans, and prefers incense and scented candles. They welcome everyone, including the neighbors, to their weekly summer barbecues and do lots of street evangelism. They tend to be young and high-tech and appreciate contemporary-style accoutrements.

At International Community Church, our service is flexible and, dare I say, fun! We laugh a lot, cry, and encourage everyone to take part. We thrive on our composition of people from many countries and cultures, stunningly evident in the communion friendship circle each month. From time to time, we vary the breads and style of communion, take a crack at learning new greetings, and attempt songs in other languages. We are told that we are friendly and hospitable with a heart for children and teens. "Lord, may it ever be so."

Collaborative feasts are the best. We swoon over each other's cuisines: Burmese noodles, Korean sushi, Caribbean jerk chicken, Chinese dumplings, Russian pastries, and even scalloped potatoes. Cathi's famous bread has become a staple, the simple recipe mastered by many. At one of our dinners, International Community Church served Fluffernutters on white bread to depict Norman Rockwell Americana. Bon appétit!

BECOMING KOREAN FOR A DAY

Hot and cold cultures are ever so distinct from each other, in cooking methods, cleaning styles, childrearing, even the pace of speaking and walking. Our northern-bred folks, accustomed to braving cold wind and snow, hustle across the floor, talk briskly, keep doors and windows closed, prefer hot water, and live more brusquely by the clock—subconsciously to keep body temperatures warm. In contrast, our tropic-bred friends, who live most of their lives in outside common areas, cook with lots of liquids that back home do not solidify for disposal, sashay through the room, speak more slowly, forget to close windows and doors, prefer cold water, and seem to have all the time in the world to converse—subconsciously to keep body temperatures cool.

And then, some cultures highly honor their elderly while others revere their young. (Where do you suppose the United States falls?) Fascinating.

The original pastor of Boston Church for Mission (Korean), Rev. Chung, founded their church on the premise that most Korean churches were enthralled with young adult culture, leaving the elderly unattended. They would, then, intentionally try to fill that gap. They would reach out to meet the needs of first-generation grandmas and grandpas who struggle to adapt to their home away from home while learning a strange language called English.

"This is a courageous vision," I thought to myself, "because growing a church on an aging population could be risky . . . but then, didn't Jesus take unprecedented risks?"

We've learned from them that Koreans bow in greeting, but not with their palms clasped together as the Chinese do. Koreans leave their arms straight at their sides. And, to an older Korean, you say, "An-ya ha-say-o," whereas to a younger Korean, "An-ya" is sufficient. I see.

On the eightieth birthday of a man in the Korean church, our two churches had planned to share lunch together.

"Give us half an hour first. On second thought, why don't your people join us? First, we will have a traditional birthday ceremony, and then we'll eat."

"Great!"

So, I did my best to prep our church for something I had never experienced. Thankfully, I thought to have us all enter the dining room in our non-customarily reserved tone and sit on the periphery, fully expecting the ceremony to be somewhat boisterous and, well, American. What was I thinking?

"Shhhhhhhhhhh."

The grandpa and his seventy-nine-year-old wife were seated at a head table with flowers and decorations all around them. A small mat was unfurled in front of them and people young and old sat facing them. Words unintelligible to our church were spoken to them, and then four men approached their table. They knelt on the rug and placed their foreheads on the floor in a gesture of utmost respect. Then another four followed.

"Shhhhhhhh," to us, the clueless quasi-Americans. "Just a few more minutes."

Then the sweet gentleman stood to the side of their table and everyone lined up to shake his hand and bow at the waist with congratulations. Remember, arms at the side. Gifts. Balloons. And food—such food, including a panda-bear-sized birthday cake. Of course, they served grandpa and grandma first, plates piled high with exquisite morsels of traditional fare. Then, we were allowed to chat and laugh and eat, something we're quite prized at.

On this day, we had been honorary Koreans-in-Boston. They had invited us into their world, and it had felt humbling. My only twinge of sadness was for those who missed this very traditional celebration. Thank you, God, for creatively creating us all.

Life is an approxamation.[1] *(Do you get it?)*

ADDITIONAL SCRIPTURES TO PONDER ON CELEBRATING OUR CULTURAL AND LINGUISTIC DISTINCTIVES

God reigns above the nations, sitting on his holy throne. The rulers of the world have gathered together with the people of the God of Abraham. For all the kings of the earth belong to God. He is highly honored everywhere. (Ps 47:8)

Everything on earth will worship you; they will sing your praises, shouting your name in glorious songs. (Ps 66:4)

---

1. Ralph Kee.

Celebrate Cultural and Linguistic Distinctives 87

Praise his glorious name forever! Let the whole earth be filled with his glory. Amen and amen! (Ps 72:19)

All the nations you made will come and bow before you, LORD; they will praise your holy name. (Ps 86:9)

The LORD will mediate between nations and will settle international disputes. (Isa 2:4)

This is what the LORD of Heaven's Armies says: In those days ten men from different nations and languages of the world will clutch at the sleeve of one Jew. And they will say, "Please let us walk with you, for we have heard that God is with you." (Zech 8:23)

After this I saw a vast crowd, too great to count, from every nation and tribe and people and language, standing in front of the throne and before the Lamb. They were clothed in white robes and held palm branches in their hands. And they were shouting with a great roar, "Salvation comes from our God who sits on the throne and from the Lamb!" And all the angels were standing around the throne and around the elders and the four living beings. And they fell before the throne with their faces to the ground and worshiped God. (Rev 7:9–11)

And I saw another angel flying through the sky, carrying the eternal Good News to proclaim to the people who belong to this world—to every nation, tribe, language, and people. "Fear God," he shouted. "Give glory to him. For the time has come when he will sit as judge. Worship him who made the heavens, the earth, the sea, and all the springs of water." (Rev 14:6–7)

15

Start Peer Learning Groups

Share each other's burdens, and in this way obey the law of Christ. If you think you are too important to help someone, you are only fooling yourself. You are not that important.

—GALATIANS 6:2

EXPERIENCING SABBATH REST

Overheard . . .

"Whew, you must have lots of money with all those groups!"

"Well, each group is . . ."

"If you had enough money, you wouldn't have to have all these groups."

"Ah, we host others not for the money, but for . . ."

"No wonder this is such a rich church. It's another sold-out show!"

"We're not . . . the headliner band requires more than . . ."

"The denomination must give you money."

"Really, we pay the deno . . ."

"You live *in* the city? The church must pay you well."

"Actually, I'm grateful for . . ."

One day, the phone rang (gotta love those phone calls) and a friend asked,

"Want to apply for a Sabbatical together? We need four pastors from Boston. How 'bout you find someone and I'll find someone. I'll email you the application. OK?"

Why not? Oooooo . . . let me check with the elders, because it looks like I could be away for some weeks. One elder promptly replied to my email, "Why are you even asking? Of *course* you should apply! And I'm praying you get it!"

The four of us began meeting to craft what we hoped would be a grant-awarded application. Before submitting it, we even covered it in Christmas wrapping paper and ribbon, a sneaky tactic to ensure that ours grabbed some attention.

Well, we did receive the Lilly Foundation grant, via Boston University School of Theology, that would reset my inner clock and forever repace my ministry life. The four of us urban pastors became fast friends in absorbing all we could about Sabbath rest, the root of the word *Sabbatical*. Initially, when we met together, we spent lots of time wading in tears for some reason. Were we that tired? We decided to study the topic of trauma and worded our required study question thus: *How can we as urban pastors be midwives of God's Sabbath rest to people who have experienced various types of trauma?* It actually became more of a prayer for us as we read and learned and interviewed experts, all the while caressing our own secondary traumas from years of ministering to the broken.

Perhaps we were a bit guarded at first, but gradually, we came to trust our quandaries to each other's confidences, prayer, and wisdom. Our theologies and views did not automatically align just because we were friends. To the contrary, we never tried to sway each other toward one understanding or the other.

It's been rather beautiful—biblical—to live out the truth that agreeing eye to eye is not synonymous with loving. This reality has possibly been our greatest lesson and our group's deepest strength: we are there for each other, cheering each other on toward healthy longevity in ministry, without requisite unanimity.

Years later, I am still retooling my praxes of Sabbath versus a day off, still grappling to work Sabbatically, stay repaced, *and* still getting together with my three Sabbatical peers. As a pastor, Sunday *is* my Sabbath, which, standing on the shoulders of Messianic Jews, I begin Saturday evening. I hustle to complete the last minutiae of preparation for Sunday before the sun sets, sometimes making it, sometimes not. But when I am finished, I clear off the kitchen table, lay out my sermon and bulletin with a candle, an angel, and my Sabbath ring. Then I call to whomever is in the house, "Ready to welcome the Sabbath?" We gather at the table, light the candle, and pray: "Lord, this is as good as it's going to get. Thank you for Jesus who is the light of the world, for the angels who minister on your behalf. May we rest deeply in your presence, now, and awake tomorrow ready to give and to receive, not out of Sunday rush, but Sabbath Rest. In Jesus' name. Amen."

In Luke 6:1–11, it was the Sabbath when Jesus received from others and gave of himself. He worshipped with the synagogue community, then taught, interacted, discerned, engaged in an unpleasant meeting of sorts, did good, and healed. Soon afterward, he took a day off for self-care and refreshment (Luke 6:12 ff).

Later in the week, I take a chunk of time off, for self-care and fun, which I encourage our church people to do as well. For how can I ask those who work five and six days a week to volunteer their energies on Sunday, if Sunday is not Sabbathly restful for both myself and them?

Recently, the Lilly Foundation concluded their decade-long project entitled *Sustaining Pastoral Excellence*—*excellence* defined as *virtue*. Having studied more than 150 grant-recipient projects—which directly influenced, they calculated, 10 percent of United States churches—they discovered the number-one factor in sustaining pastoral excellence.[1] You know what it is? Take a guess. *Peer learning groups!* And

1. Miller, *Sustaining Pastoral Excellence*.

guess what inherent gift awaits pastors who collaborate in Christian ministry? *Peers!*

I reported their findings at a subsequent interchurch council, that regular gathering for pastors and leaders collaborating in our setting. Then I put out the question, "Do you have a group of pastoral peers?"

One said, "Yes. I meet with pastors from my denomination once a month."

"And I have a group of four friends in ministry with whom I can share freely."

Two pastors were absent. But the third, to my surprise, interjected,

"This is my most authentic peer group, right here with all of you."

I was stunned, not sure whether to be pleased or reproved. I've always tried to structure our meetings with what seemed to be proper priorities: devotions, then ministry updates—*Where is God working in your group, in you?*—then planning, and property matters last before ending in a time of prayer. The majority of interchurch councils have been uplifting, like a mini-retreat. But I realized my brother was on to something.

Occasionally, I discover that a leader in our midst holds a view divergent from mine regarding women in key pastoral roles, even though he must relate to me as overseeing pastor. Years ago, I participated in a pastors' peer learning group where it was always "Lorraine and the guys." One of my friends quietly stayed home during my ordination council and ceremony, but invited me to preach for him when he was on vacation. Our differing views have never once interfered with our friendship or our ability for fellowship in Christ. Still, we do not have to agree; we only need to covenant to love one another in the same way that Jesus loves us.

I hope now that we can take our interchurch council gatherings to the next level and intentionally deepen our collegiality, learning, vulnerability, prayer, and support. Can we mirror Lilly's findings in our context for even truer collaborative ministry? Can we learn and grow together?

There is too much at stake not to try.

A compliment is a kiss from God.[2]

ADDITIONAL SCRIPTURES TO PONDER ON SUSTAINING PASTORAL EXCELLENCE THROUGH COLLABORATIVE PEER GROUPS

After David had finished talking with Saul, he met Jonathan, the king's son. There was an immediate bond between them. (1 Sam 18:1)

A person standing alone can be attacked and defeated, but two can stand back-to-back and conquer. Three are even better, for a triple-braided cord is not easily broken. (Eccl 4:12)

"Look!" Nebuchadnezzar shouted. "I see four men, unbound, walking around in the fire unharmed! And the fourth looks like a god!" Then Nebuchadnezzar came as close as he could to the door of the flaming furnace and shouted: "Shadrach, Meshach, and

---

2. Diane C.

Abednego, servants of the Most High God, come out! (Dan 3:25–26)

These are the twelve [Jesus] chose: Simon (whom he named Peter), James and John (the sons of Zebedee, but Jesus nicknamed them "Sons of Thunder"), Andrew, Philip, Bartholomew, Matthew, Thomas, James (son of Alphaeus), Thaddaeus, Simon (the zealot), Judas Iscariot (who later betrayed him). (Mark 3:16–19)

That Sunday evening the disciples were meeting behind locked doors. (John 20:19)

Then the apostles returned to Jerusalem from the Mount of Olives, a distance of half a mile. When they arrived, they went to the upstairs room of the house where they were staying. Here are the names of those who were present: Peter, John, James, Andrew, Philip, Thomas, Bartholomew, Matthew, James (son of Alphaeus), Simon (the Zealot), and Judas (son of James). They all met together and were constantly united in prayer, along with Mary the mother of Jesus, several other women, and the brothers of Jesus. (Acts 1:12–14)

On the day of Pentecost all the believers were meeting together in one place. Suddenly, there was a sound from heaven. (Acts 2:1)

16

Hang World Maps and International Art

For God loved the world so much that he gave his one and only Son, so that everyone who believes in him will not perish but have eternal life.

—JOHN 3:16

AFIRMING OUR VARIOUS CULTURES

New Life Church's gigantic world map, which wallpapered a whole corner of the room, had become a favorite hangout spot.

"Where are you from?"

"Mmmm, right about here. No, here."

"And where is Belize? Africa?"

So, it was natural when we formed ICC to overlay one wall with a similar map. One glitch: the walls are stucco, and nothing adheres or mounts easily. We began, therefore, to hang dry-mounted world maps from picture rails just below the ceilings. There's the correctly proportioned United Nations Development Program Map in the sanctuary, the bright blue map with national flags in the children's room, a little pale colored one on the landing, the Burma-shaped clock whose battery is continually lazy in the little chapel, and, of course, the roving globe.

For me, the globe is ideally perched on the altar, cradling our prayers and our people, echoing the song lyrics, "He's got the whole world in his hands." But you might find it anywhere.

For years, I've mimicked a repetitious cuckoo chime, requesting international pictures of Jesus and nationals as well as art representing other cultures, but, alas, it hasn't caught on.

When Jean Ehsay passed away,[1] her church bought a Burmese tabletop cross in her honor. When we set up for a second, simultaneous worship service, one of us grabs the Burmese cross to create an altar. It's gold with cobalt blue-

1. See chapter 9.

and-white figures soldered to its four points: an angel, a lion, an eagle, and a bull. A lamb prominently covers the cross's intersection, and Jean's name is engraved delicately on its base. Two small banners of Psalm 23, hand-embroidered in Burmese and English by our dear Mr. Htoo, hang in one of the lobbies. They are black with gold lettering and a picture of Jesus cradling a lamb. When I visited Burma, he insisted I bring them back for the church.

Jack's[2] heavy, metal-studded, gray, red-centered cross graces a back table, which we always display during Holy Week. It's particularly poignant to place it low enough for people to run their hands across, carefully, as it can cut. Piquant. One of his art forms incorporated bits of refuse from the streets, so he signed his work "Jacques Debris." A brilliant artist.

The Russian church brings out their clusters of candles each week, creating an Eastern European ambiance for a few hours. And upstairs, their pastor's tongue-in-cheek sign by his desk declares, "Parking for Estonians Only."

The Deaf church keeps their space adorned with a hand-drawn picture of Jesus and the universal *I love you* sign.

Together, our churches made a quilted wall-hanging which states in various languages, *God is. . . .* Each church permanent-markered their description of God on one square. The final patch completes the opening sentence: *. . . Jesus*, as explained by Colossians 2:9: "For in Christ lives all the fullness of God in a human body." It's artistically done, simple, framed in African cloth, linguistically specific, and

2. See chapter 1.

affixed where a well-worn poster of the International Last Supper used to be.

Down a bit from our homespun mini-tapestry hangs a hand-painted picture of Jesus strolling through Oicha, Congo, with a frail, sickly woman straining to touch the hem of his garment. The artist, Kahi, was our interpreter several years back, and had at that time never traveled more than thirty kilometers from his village. He uses leftover house paints with remarkable acumen.

The children's room displays an old picture of Jesus surrounded by the children of the world, cherished by the oldest member of our church.

In the sanctuary and adjoining rooms, there are Bibles and hymnbooks in English, Korean, Chinese, Burmese, and Russian, as well as fliers and notices and mailings targeting specific demographics. One back closet still shelves a Braille Bible that isn't often used because of its sheer bulkiness, now replaced by advanced technological aids for the blind.

The yard sign announces all of our churches and groups equally. We each have one slat containing three lines: the name of our church in our native language, our primary gathering time, and web site or phone.

Several summers ago, ten international high school students stayed in our homes and used our church as their home base while interacting with American culture and improving their English. Stacey, one of our young adult members, was their coordinator and tutor throughout their three-week stay in Boston. One of their projects was the brainchild of Sidewalk Sam, an iconic local street artist befriended to us through Jack. He led them in painting the city's first Dove of Peace on our front walkway while engaging them in conversations about international peace and self-initiative. The dove is about a yard square and heralds the ribboned message, "Create Peace, Stop Violence." Similar doves can be spotted all over the city, tragically at locales of recent homicides.

The church's resident-custodians sometimes work around while wearing their *longees* (a Burmese wrap) and flip-flops, the older Russian women wear long skirts and headscarves in the cold, and the Deaf always attract attention when they're signing together on the lawn.

Sigh. Still, I wish I could get our churches to display art from their countries so we could better appreciate each other's cultures.

So, why don't they?

Art is the soul in paint.

ADDITIONAL SCRIPTURES TO PONDER ON DISPLAYING CULTURALLY SENSITIVE ART AND MAPS

At that time there were devout Jews from every nation living in Jerusalem. When they heard the loud noise, everyone came running, and they were bewildered to hear their own languages being spoken by the believers. They were completely amazed. "How can this be?" they exclaimed. "These people are all from Galilee, and yet we hear them speaking in our own native languages! Here we are—Parthians, Medes, Elamites, people from Mesopotamia, Judea, Cappadocia, Pontus, the province of Asia, Phrygia, Pamphylia, Egypt, and the areas of Libya around Cyrene, visitors from Rome (both Jews and converts to Judaism), Cretans, and Arabs. And we all hear these people speaking in our own languages about the wonderful things God has done!" (Acts 2:5–11)

The next day as Cornelius's messengers were nearing the town, Peter went up on the flat roof to pray. It was about noon, and he was hungry. But while a meal was being prepared, he fell into a trance. He saw the sky open, and something like a large sheet was let down by its four corners. In the sheet were all sorts of animals, reptiles, and birds. Then a voice said to him, "Get up, Peter; kill and eat them." "No, Lord," Peter declared. "I have never eaten anything that our Jewish laws have declared impure and unclean." But the voice spoke again: "Do not call something unclean if God has made it clean." The same vision was repeated three times. Then the sheet was suddenly pulled up to heaven. Peter was very perplexed. What could the vision mean? . . . They arrived in Caesarea the following day. Cornelius was waiting for them and had called together his relatives and close friends. As Peter entered his home, Cornelius fell at his feet and worshiped him. But Peter pulled him up and said, "Stand up! I'm a human being just like you!" So they talked together and went inside, where many others were assembled. Peter told them, "You know it is against our laws for a Jewish man to enter a Gentile home like this or to associate with you. But God has shown me that I should no longer think of anyone as impure or unclean." (Acts 10:9–17, 24–28; try to read Acts 10 and 11 in their entirety.)

17

Pray! Pray! Pray!

*Before daybreak the next morning, Jesus got up
and went out to an isolated place to pray.*

—MARK 1:35

BATHE IT ALL IN PRAYER

We were a pastoral team of three: Ralph, Judy, and me. During our biweekly meetings, Ralph and I were full speed ahead—brainstorming, planning, programming, scheduling. Judy would mumble and interject dolefully until she couldn't stand it any longer. Scrambling for her church directory, she would rustle through its pages: "The people. What about the people and the families? When are we going to talk about *them*?"

I remember the first time she did this, I was taken aback, half scolding myself, half scolding her, talking to myself.

"I thought we were . . . isn't all this about the people?"

But Judy pressed us. "Let's go down through the directory and update ourselves on their needs so we can pray more intelligently."

Judy taught me to focus on individuals. Because of her, I have made it my habit to pray through the directory nearly every Sunday morning before church. ("Nearly" because . . . well, it never seems nearly enough.)

Our interchurch councils always include prayer, but not nearly enough. For a couple of years, we met during Lent with people from our collaborative churches to pray in front of a world map. One person would select a country and begin praying, then others would join in until we all felt satisfied with our prayer coverage for that region. Then, someone else would mention or point to another country and initiate group prayer for that area, and so on. Much of the globe was represented among us, so we prayed for our world, but not nearly enough.

Our own church has tried many different ways to gather in prayer: 9:30 Sundays in the balcony, Wednesday evenings with dinner, Thursday evenings without dinner, pastors' prayer days at camp, prayer meetings in our home, prayer meetings in someone else's home, prayer walks, prayer in the little chapel at 9:00 Sundays, ecumenical prayer vigils, and, of late, home prayer visits once a week. Judy is the queen of telephone prayers, reminding us to pray with each other spontaneously over the phone. I often pray in emails—*Reply* or *Reply to All*—lest I forget someone's appeal. We've had some success, but not nearly enough.

Immanuel Deaf Church prays every Saturday evening, Boston Church for Mission (Korean) prays every Thursday at 5:30 a.m. [that's a.m., not p.m.], Overseas Burmese Christian Fellowship prays weekly in homes, our church likewise prays in homes, Grace Church (Russian) prays on Friday evenings during Bible Study. We leave time during interchurch councils to pray for each other's people. Of course, there is prayer during every worship service, often anointing people with oil and lingering in special prayer, as when Teen Challenge visits. We pray during Kids for Christ, during Sunday Schools, before meals, with newly arrived folks, and with people saying goodbye. All of us pray in our cars, on the subway, as we walk, before we sleep, when we awake, before exams, after achievements. We are all praying, but not nearly enough.

Paulo, who came to one of the Brazilian churches in our building years ago, still swings by just about every day to pray. Between his miniscule, heroic English and my five

Portuguese words, we pantomime through our family news together, but our prayer languages require no translation when, once in a while, I join him. But generally it's Paulo and Jesus. On Sundays, I watch him kneel by the pew with his Bible, sing praises to his Lord, then lift his hands in prayer. I always say, "Obrigado, Paulo. Please pray for all our churches too." "Yes. Okay," his brown-toothed smile broadening with faith. One dear man of God seems not nearly enough.

When language fails, I groan two prayers: the one recited by Catholics, "Lord, have mercy," and the prayer that never fails, "Thy will be done."

A PRAYER SURGE

On the other end of the phone was a man inquiring if we might be able to host a group of students. They were from International House of Prayer University and were coming to Boston for forty days to fast and pray for our city.

"How many?"

"Over a hundred. We've found accommodations for all but forty guys."

"Well, we have lots of hard floor space. If they bring their sleeping bags, store them during the day, and take showers at the YMCA, maybe we can work it out."

So they came. Laptops, sleeping bags, inflatable mattresses, cell phones, chargers, duffle bags, tortilla chips for their nonfasting hours. It was Lent, and they flooded our space with guy stuff and prayer, much prayer. They prayer-walked the city streets, encouraged believers, introduced nonbelievers to Christ, sang, and prayed every evening in another church. I joined them twice and was not surprised to discover they were charismatic in style, filled with Holy Spirit faith, and eager to pray for one another. Resolve deepened dramatically among these young adults, reminding me of the Haystack meetings in Northampton two centuries ago. Just after Easter, three hundred additional students joined them for one last week of prayer-surge. The contagion of their prayer lives infiltrated churches, schools, businesses, government buildings, and universities across the city, whether their occupants were aware of it or not. Cold and driving rain did not derail their efforts. They prayed fervently and plan to return within a few years, because forty days, they decried, was not enough. I'm counting down the months.

May we never be so arrogant that we forge ahead prayerless. May we never be so spiritual that we pray through actionless.

Oh, God, is it enough?

> *Those who receive individual attention, thrive.*
> *Those who don't, don't—not nearly enough.*

ADDITIONAL SCRIPTURES TO PONDER ON PRAYING, PRAYING, PRAYING

On the morning of the third day, thunder roared and lightning flashed, and a dense cloud came down on the mountain. There was a long, loud blast from a ram's horn, and all the people trembled. Moses led them out from the camp to meet with God, and they stood at the foot of the mountain. All of Mount Sinai was covered with smoke because the LORD had descended on it in the form of fire. The smoke billowed into the sky like smoke from a brick kiln, and the whole mountain shook violently. As the blast of the ram's horn grew louder and louder, Moses spoke, and God thundered his reply. (Exod 19:16–19)

Accept my prayer as incense offered to you, and my upraised hands as an evening offering. (Ps 141:2)

Then Jonah prayed to the LORD his God from inside the fish. He said, "I cried out to the LORD in my great trouble, and he answered me. (Jonah 2:1)

Pray for those who persecute you! (Matt 5:44)

When you pray, don't be like the hypocrites who love to pray publicly on street corners and in the synagogues where everyone can see them. I tell you the truth, that is all the reward they will ever get. But when you pray, go away by yourself, shut the door behind you, and pray to your Father in private. Then your Father, who sees everything, will reward you. When you pray, don't babble on and on as people of other religions do. They think their prayers are answered merely by repeating their words again and again. Don't be like them, for your Father knows exactly what you need even before you ask him! Pray like this: *Our Father in heaven, may your name be kept holy. May your Kingdom come soon. May your will be done on earth, as it is in heaven. Give us today the food we need, and forgive us our sins, as we have forgiven those who sin against us. And don't let us yield to temptation, but rescue us from the evil one.* (Matt 6:5–18)

After this prayer, the meeting place shook, and they were all filled with the Holy Spirit. (Acts 4:31)

And the Holy Spirit helps us in our weakness. For example, we don't know what God wants us to pray for. But the Holy Spirit prays for us with groanings that cannot be expressed in words. (Rom 8:26)

Pray in the Spirit at all times and on every occasion. Stay alert and be persistent in your prayers for all believers everywhere. And pray for me, too. (Eph 6:18)

Never stop praying. (1 Thess 5:17)

Timothy, I thank God for you—the God I serve with a clear conscience, just as my ancestors did. Night and day I constantly remember you in my prayers. (2 Tim 1:3)

18

Play! Play! Play!

When Jesus came by, he looked up at Zacchaeus and called him by name. "Zacchaeus!" he said. "Quick, come down! I must be a guest in your home today." Zacchaeus quickly climbed down and took Jesus to his house in great excitement and joy!

—LUKE 19:5–6

LET THE FUN BEGIN

Fireworks and balloons feel so appropriate in church—though the former we have yet to implement. Sometimes, I feel perfectly giddy as church unfolds, watching the Holy Spirit affect lives and people connect with their God.

Separate, our churches are silver; together, they are gold.

Twice, we held a daylong collaborative festival called "Church Is Fun." All the churches participated in blocking off the street (obtaining city permits is a full-time job, by the way), playing Burmese ball, Brazilian soccer, jump-rope, volleyball (oops—one window down), chalk drawings, barbecue, yard sale/giveaway, car wash, water sprinkler, and, of course, a brief worship with international music. What fun, although one cab nearly crashed into the light pole when he spotted the sign "FREE."

We covenant to hold at least one collaborative event each year, but due to random work schedules, people miss out. Therefore, in addition to our combined annual service, each church plans its own celebrations and usually invites the others to participate.

For example, the Burmese Food Fair provides a fun-loving occasion to mingle and sample the real deal, Burmese food, and to wear our Asian garb. Traditional Burmese dancing is riveting.

The Deaf celebrate their church anniversary each fall and always invite everyone to share their joy. Generally, they perform a drama, sing, and enjoy hair-raising preaching. Just to be present is a cross-cultural experience of deep profundity.

The Russian church has been casually grilling up a storm of high-quality burgers and dogs with an open invitation for free food, followed by nourishing Bible study and prayer. Real good! We've got our eyes peeled for that cab driver.

The Korean youth chamber orchestra performed in a nursing home around the corner where sick older folks beamed at the young talent directed their way. Another church tagged along too.

ICC has hosted After-Supper Bible Camp one summer's week for many years, the most exhaustingly exhilarating week of the fifty-two! Children from the neighborhood are always invited, but most come from our collaborative churches, infusing our kids with another rich bolus of cross-cultural Christian friends. Besides the obvious goal of introducing them to Jesus Christ and growing them in him, we want more than anything else for our children and teens to love coming to church. We want church to be a blast: more exciting than baseball, more comforting than ice cream, more fulfilling than Narnia . . . or at least, as fulfilling.

Our churches have together worshipped, mourned, married, sung, preached, baptized, communed, and prayed. But when we play together, we become on the inside what Jesus treasured: little children playing together at his feet, safe, loved, content, and free.

> *Don't just work at building healthy relationships,*
> *play at it!*

ADDITIONAL SCRIPTURES TO PONDER ON PLAYING, PLAYING, PLAYING

And Nehemiah continued, "Go and celebrate with a feast of rich foods and sweet drinks, and share gifts of food with people who have nothing prepared. This is a sacred day before our Lord. Don't be dejected and sad, for the joy of the Lord is your strength!" (Neh 8:10)

You satisfy me more than the richest feast. I will praise you with songs of joy. I lie awake thinking of you, meditating on you through the night. Because you are my helper, I sing for joy in the shadow of your wings. (Ps 63:5–7)

But let the godly rejoice. Let them be glad in God's presence. Let them be filled with joy. Sing praises to God and to his name! Sing loud praises to him who rides the clouds. His name is the Lord—rejoice in his presence! (Ps 68:3–4)

Joyful indeed are those whose God is the Lord! (Ps 144:15)

A cheerful heart is good medicine, but a broken spirit saps a person's strength. (Prov 17:22)

Later, Matthew invited Jesus and his disciples to his home as dinner guests, along with many tax collectors and other disreputable sinners. (Matt 9:10)

One day some parents brought their little children to Jesus so he could touch and bless them. But when the disciples saw this, they scolded the parents for bothering him. Then Jesus called for the children and said to the disciples, "Let the children come to me. Don't stop them! For the Kingdom of God belongs to those who are like these children. I tell you the truth, anyone who doesn't receive the Kingdom of God like a child will never enter it." (Luke 18:15–17)

The next day there was a wedding celebration in the village of Cana in Galilee. Jesus' mother was there, and Jesus and his disciples were also invited to the celebration. (John 2:1–2)

19

Stay! Stay! Stay!

So, my dear brothers and sisters, be strong and immovable. Always work enthusiastically for the Lord, for you know that nothing you do for the Lord is ever useless.

—1 CORINTHIANS 15:58

IN IT FOR THE LONG HAUL

Sir Winston Churchill said it best when he addressed a British high school. He had been allotted about twenty minutes, so stood at the podium, galvanized his gaze, and advised the student body,

"Never give up. Never, never, *never* give up!" Then he sat down.

At my ordination, I asked my dear friend Judy Hall to give the Charge to the Ordinand. All I remember was her cautioning me not to leave Boston, because, she alleged,

"The city needs us."

Was she detecting my soul's longing for home, the coast of my beloved Maine? No worries. God had already dropped anchor in urban waters for me, not in just any city, but this one specifically—Boston, Massachusetts.

Boston was a harsher place when I first arrived as a student in the sixties. We would drive in from Wenham, a rural town thirty miles to the north, every Friday night to hold services and prepare dinner for Calvary Rescue Mission. Honestly, we were fearless. We'd sing at the top of our lungs and pray as soon as we hit the city line of Lynn just outside Boston, my heart throbbing with anticipation, and always God would answer our prayer for a parking spot.

We'd go right into the bars and scold the guys, "What are you doing in here? Come on, it's time for service!"

And they'd follow us, who were just kids to them. Dave Elder would stand night after night with tears drenching his handsome, alcohol-destroyed face and quote from the King James Version, Psalm 119:165:

"Great peace have they which love Thy law, O LORD, and nothing shall offend them."

And then there was Maurice, a tall Canadian man with puckered acne scars, sweet, polite, very alcoholic. Week after week, someone from our group would pay two dollars so he could sleep next door in that roach-dominated excuse for a hotel.

Once I had an armload of frozen shrimp stew to prepare for the guests. When I dropped it into the sink at Calvary, the impact rattled the dirty yellow wainscoting and it turned black for a split second with roaches jarred from the crevices. This was the sixties version of today's various ministries to the "unhoused," living on the streets of our cities.

We were undeterred students embracing the shock of inner-city drudgery and beauty with a sense of awe and honor and horror. Yes, I was feeling called here.

Then, later, when I married my college sweetheart, we worked alongside Rev. Ralph Kee at South End Neighborhood Church. Girls for God, the MOMS Group (Management of Mayhem, Sometimes), youth group, Bible studies, and all the rest. Yes, we would stay here.

And when our son was born, I recall holding him on the couch blubbering, "I don't know how to raise a son in the city!" How can I let him go and run and climb and ride his bike in our sketchy neighborhood?

But then, I would see the faces of urban ministry friends from way back, like Doug, Ralph, Chet, Joanne, Marilyn. And I'd recall people like Ken, Priscilla, Helen, Doris, Mrs. Atlas, Roy, Ethel, Claire, Eddie, Floyd, even Roscoe—the rascal who stole my new Bible—and Miss Hobley. And, of course, the kids like Donna, Michael, Jay,

Juggy, Lovell, Sandy, Patrice, Kim, and many more. There was no question that we were in this for the long haul.

Many years. At times, I have felt my cup leaking. That's when I pray the song, "Fill my cup, Lord, I lift it up, Lord; come and quench this thirsting of my soul. Bread of heaven, feed me 'til I want no more. Here's my cup, fill it up and make me whole."[1]

And God does. Over and over.

Yes, because he has stayed, I have stayed.

MISSION STATEMENTS FOR LONG-TERM MINISTRY

International Community Church has three statements that, we pray, stabilize the grid and supply the grist for long-time *staying* ministry:

(1) Our *purpose* is to introduce people to Jesus Christ, to grow them in him, and to send them out.

(2) Our *vision* is to be a flexible, ever-changing urban church that develops young leaders, pastors people in smaller groups, and hosts churches and organizations. A second-layer vision is like it: We will join others in impacting a cultural shift toward Christianity through real community, real hospitality, real communication, real Messiah, and real relevance.

(3) We *focus* on the One, the Word, and the world.

Fierce loyalty.[2]

---

1 Words and music by Richard Blanchard, 1964.
2 Joanne Kee.

ADDITIONAL SCRIPTURES TO PONDER ON LONGEVITY IN COLLABORATIVE MINISTRY

The Lord is good to those who depend on him, to those who search for him. So it is good to wait quietly for salvation from the Lord. And it is good for people to submit at an early age to the yoke of his discipline. (Lam 3:25–27)

Remain in me, and I will remain in you. For a branch cannot produce fruit if it is severed from the vine, and you cannot be fruitful unless you remain in me. Yes, I am the vine; you are the branches. Those who remain in me, and I in them, will produce much fruit. For apart from me you can do nothing. (John 15:4–5)

Let the Spirit renew your thoughts and attitudes. (Eph 4:23)

Stand your ground, putting on the belt of truth and the body armor of God's righteousness. (Eph 6:14)

Don't be selfish; don't try to impress others. Be humble, thinking of others as better than yourselves. Don't look out only for your own interests, but take an interest in others, too. You must have the same attitude that Christ Jesus had. (Phil 2:3–5)

And now, dear brothers and sisters, one final thing. Fix your thoughts on what is true, and honorable, and right, and pure, and lovely, and admirable. Think about things that are excellent and worthy of praise. Keep putting into practice all you learned and received from me—everything you heard from me and saw me doing. Then the God of peace will be with you. (Phil 4:8–9)

> Think about the things of heaven, not the things of earth. For you died to this life, and your real life is hidden with Christ in God. And when Christ, who is your life, is revealed to the whole world, you will share in all his glory. So put to death the sinful, earthly things lurking within you. (Col 3:2–5)

20

Leave Well

Then Jesus led them to Bethany, and lifting his hands to heaven, he blessed them. While he was blessing them, he left them and was taken up to heaven. So they worshiped him and then returned to Jerusalem filled with great joy. And they spent all of their time in the Temple, praising God.

—LUKE 24:50–53

GRACE IN GOODBYES

Ai Doh had been in the States nearly eight years acquiring higher theological degrees, living in various dormitories. But now that he was no longer a student, he needed a place off campus.

"May I live as a resident-custodian in the church until I leave?"

There are always loose ends to tie up before leaving a country: passports, visas, closing of bank accounts, earning enough to pay off remaining bills, traveling to other states for final farewells, accumulating gifts to distribute back home, shipping books ahead—the list is endless and requires every last day allotted on a visa by our government.

"If there's enough space in the guys' room, and if you can devote ten hours a week to chores, sure."

Our resident-custodians live rent-free for in-kind payment in the form of cleaning, security, hosting, you name it. Their presence is critical in maintaining a radically hospitable atmosphere in the building because, often, they are front-line greeters. As I remind them, they are the face of Jesus to whoever rings that bell. And, of course, they can't be cleaning up after a group whom they resent for being sloppy, that's for sure. So praying as they putter and whistling while they work is key.

Ai Doh moved in and not only tackled his assigned duties, but added to them, as other resident-custodians had done before him. Why have we not yet come up with the technology to clone the best among us?

All too soon, however, everything on his list was checked off and his journey home was imminent. Ai Doh began thanking individuals, encouraging our collaborative churches, rehearsing the ups and downs of his years here, laughing and lamenting, and analyzing his own maturation. For several months, he gradually withdrew his inner energy from Boston and transferred it to Burma. As far as I could ascertain, when he boarded his flight, there were no gifts left unopened or withheld, no resentments, no unspoken apologies, no hidden agendas, no regrets, no dangling celebrations. Amazing. Because he had said a thoroughly careful goodbye, he could say a full-hearted hello back home.

Tragically, stories of poor or no goodbyes at all are far more common. There was the church that, after more than ten years of sharing space with us, simply left a voice mail on a Wednesday to inform us that they were moving out, effective immediately. They retrieved their sound equipment the following Saturday, but left the bulk of their supplies behind for us either to use or discard. I called and called, urging them to come back and say goodbye rather than leave us all wondering what happened. Did someone offend them? Did their schedule need adjusting? Was their storage space inadequate? All these pieces lay chipped and broken, strewn on the floor of our collective memories. Years later, I still experience a twitch when I notice their Sunday School materials in the teen center. A hospitable goodbye—God-graced closure—could have allayed this residue of grief and tension.

Church folk are notorious for suddenly disappearing.

"By the way, I haven't seen the Trundles lately, have you?"

It seems harmless enough, but a minor scratch, uncleaned, festers into an oozing, painful wound. On the other hand, when a whole church or organization leaves poorly, things go unsaid, beaches uncombed. Christian collaboration always includes vulnerability of the most sacred kind because we entrust our minds and hearts to each other. Inept closure not only sours us, but damages trust, and just plain hurts.

And when it is time to say goodbye for whatever reason, the past does not need to be trashed or vilified. Rather, it needs to be held appreciatively, honored, and saved to our inner hard-drives as a lifelong resource.

Leaving well, especially among Christians, allows relationships to remain intact, unharmed, wrapped in the same love with which Jesus loves us.

> *Be twice as hospitable in saying goodbye*
> *as in saying hello.*

ADDITIONAL SCRIPTURES TO PONDER ON GOD-GRACED CLOSURE

Don't sin by letting anger control you. Think about it overnight and remain silent. (Ps 4:4)

It is not an enemy who taunts me—I could bear that. It is not my foes who so arrogantly insult me—I could have hidden from them. Instead, it is you—my equal, my companion and close friend. What good fellowship we once enjoyed as we walked together to the house of God. (Ps 55:12–14)

There is more than enough room in my Father's home. If this were not so, would I have told you that I am going to prepare a place for you? When everything is ready,

I will come and get you, so that you will always be with me where I am. (John 14:2–3)

After some time Paul said to Barnabas, "Let's go back and visit each city where we previously preached the word of the Lord, to see how the new believers are doing." Barnabas agreed and wanted to take along John Mark. But Paul disagreed strongly, since John Mark had deserted them in Pamphylia and had not continued with them in their work. Their disagreement was so sharp that they separated. Barnabas took John Mark with him and sailed for Cyprus. (Acts 15:36–39)

Don't just pretend to love others. Really love them. Hate what is wrong. Hold tightly to what is good. Love each other with genuine affection, and take delight in honoring each other. Never be lazy, but work hard and serve the Lord enthusiastically. Rejoice in our confident hope. Be patient in trouble, and keep on praying. When God's people are in need, be ready to help them. Always be eager to practice hospitality. Bless those who persecute you. Don't curse them; pray that God will bless them. Be happy with those who are happy, and weep with those who weep. Live in harmony with each other. Don't be too proud to enjoy the company of ordinary people. And don't think you know it all! Never pay back evil with more evil. Do things in such a way that everyone can see you are honorable. Do all that you can to live in peace with everyone. Dear friends, never take revenge. Leave that to the righteous anger of God. For the Scriptures say, "I will take revenge; I will pay them back," says the Lord. Instead,

> "If your enemies are hungry, feed them. If they are thirsty, give them something to drink. In doing this, you will heap burning coals of shame on their heads." Don't let evil conquer you, but conquer evil by doing good. (Rom 12:9–21)

> But now let me show you a way of life that is best of all. If I could speak all the languages of earth and of angels, but didn't love others, I would only be a noisy gong or a clanging cymbal. If I had the gift of prophecy, and if I understood all of God's secret plans and possessed all knowledge, and if I had such faith that I could move mountains, but didn't love others, I would be nothing. If I gave everything I have to the poor and even sacrificed my body, I could boast about it; but if I didn't love others, I would have gained nothing. (1 Cor 12:31–13:3)

Postscript

MY HUSBAND was at the wheel as we drove across one of our favorite crescent-shaped bridges high above the Piscataqua River. It was evening, and the sun had set moments before. The sheer height of the structure permitted an unobstructed view far into the New Hampshire and southern Maine mountains.

I glanced out at the canvas below and spotted a lone motor boat speeding into the sunset. There was a couple, leaning toward each other, obviously lovers enthralled with the unfolding vista enveloping them. The colors were striking: burnt orange, yolk yellow, fire-engine red, midnight black, and chandelier crystal.

Then I noticed the wake. It was wavy, almost lacy, half the width of the stern at its origin, then expanding exponentially as its intensity gentled and rippled from shoreline to shoreline. The sun was dribbling its rays like a basketball off the peaks of the wake, radiating diamonds of sunbeams. It was a breathtaking sight.

The couple was, quite naturally, focused on the view ahead of them, steering their boat down river, absorbed in each other. Maybe they were deciding on names for their children or planning their retirement.

But what riveted my attention was the superlative they were unwittingly creating. They were, rightfully so, oblivious to the radiant trail behind their vessel as they sped forward.

As we speed into the future, when we rest deeply in the Lord and let him teach us how to welcome the stranger, how to move over, how to see the invisible—the overlooked—maybe, by God's grace, our churches too will unwittingly leave a wake behind them of magnificent brilliance.

May we share far more than just kitchens and rooms under one steeple, in our churches. Rather, may we revel deeply in the rich treasures of give and take, learning and teaching, yes and no, apology and forgiveness—the robe that Jesus wore and now holds for us to adorn.

Hospiradicality, in Jesus' name.

> *"Now which of these three would you say was a neighbor to the man who was attacked by bandits?" Jesus asked. The man replied, "The one who showed him mercy." Then Jesus said, "Yes, now go and do the same." (Luke 10:36-37)*

Appendix A

Covenant for Shared Space

Pastor or Leader:

Name _____

Home Address _____

Phones _____

Email _____

Website _____

International Community Church—American Baptist [ICC] joyfully covenants with

_____

[name of church/group]

for purposes of Christian ministry.

ICC covenants to:

1. Be sure all churches lift high the person and work of Jesus Christ, the authority of Scripture, and Christlike love for one another.
2. Pray for you.
3. Respect your distinctives and strive to love as Jesus has loved us. (John 13:34)
4. Share our space, furniture, and belongings gladly.
5. Provide you an office cubicle.
6. Provide one or more storage areas. Rooms are for people; closets/cabinets for stuff.
7. Post a quarterly master calendar. Your color is _____, and orange affects all.
8. Facilitate regular interchurch councils for leaders.
9. Collaborate in at least one, annual interchurch worship and feast.
10. Participate in as many of your events as possible.
11. Oversee Residents who clean, manage trash, and check windows and doors nightly.
12. Provide a teen center and children's room, to be used *only under supervision of a responsible adult.*
13. Offer one, one-way driveway, accommodating five closely parked cars.
14. Offer one slat on the external sign, at your expense.
15. Provide one mailbox per group and one set of keys, which you may duplicate with discretion.

Appendix A 129

16. Be sure that you and all groups have attached proof of individual church insurance. This is mandatory.
17. If and when a church/group relocates, we will say good-bye Christianly (Acts 1) and help them to leave well.

_____ covenants to:
[name of church or group]

1. Lift high the person and work of Jesus Christ, the authority of Scripture, and Christlike love for one another.
2. Pray for the other churches/groups.
3. Respect the distinctives of others and strive to love as Jesus has loved us. (John 13:34)
4. Share ICC's space, furniture, and belongings gladly. When something breaks, we will repair or replace it, within reason, and leave rooms ready for the next group.
5. Pay our monthly shared expenses to the ICC Treasurer the first of each month in the amount of $_____.
6. Restrict our exclusive belongings to our designated storage, noting that items in common areas are used in common.
7. Clean and update our magnets on the quarterly master calendar. Our color is _____.

8. Participate in interchurch councils, bringing an interpreter, if needed.

9. Participate in at least one interchurch worship/feast each year.

10. Participate in as many events sponsored by our collaborative churches/groups as possible, lending encouragement and prayer.

11. Be absolutely sure that all candles are extinguished, electronics are off, and windows and doors are locked before leaving.

12. Keep children and teens safe by strictly adhering to KWAAAT: Kids With Adults At All Times.

13. Park in the neighborhood; not driving across grass or parking in our neighbors' driveway. We further covenant to be the face of Jesus within the neighborhood.

14. Advertise our events while promoting our collaborative churches as well, putting others before ourselves. (Phil 2)

15. Care for the building as though it were ours, distributing keys with discretion; treat those who enter— the stranger and the known—as though they were family.

16. Attach proof of our church insurance, realizing we cannot join this space without insurance coverage. It is mandatory.

17. If and when we relocate, we will say goodbye Christianly (Acts 1) and leave well.

We share together in the work of Jesus Christ and, above all else, seek to encourage each other in doing his will (Rom 12). We will do our best to create an environment reflecting God's peace (Phil 4:4–7) and be known by our love for one another (2 Cor 8:24). Peace to this house (Luke 10:5).

Signed _____
[authorized Church/Group Signature]

Signed _____
[authorized ICC Signature]

Today's Date _____

Appendix B

Covenant for Resident-Custodians

Name _____

Telephone _____

Email _____

Name of the Church _____

Name of the Pastor _____

International Community Church joyfully enters into covenant with _____ in a "Room for Service Exchange" for the purposes of Christian ministry.

I, _____,
agree to the following:

1. I will negotiate my responsibilities with designated person(s) of International Community Church.
2. I will serve minimum of ten hours per week in exchange for bedroom and bathroom availability and shared use of the kitchen.

3. I will conduct myself in a manner honoring the God we serve, maintaining my own spiritual and personal life with care.
4. Aware that the stranger and the hurting often enter here, I will do my best to encounter each individual with kindness and respect.
5. With God's help, I will do all in my power to protect the people and property of this building.
6. As many diverse churches and parachurch ministries share this building, by God's grace, I will do all I can to create a welcoming atmosphere reflecting the peace and love of Jesus Christ.
7. I will sign the Liability Waiver, releasing International Community Church of all forms of personal liability.
8. I understand that I am not responsible for building use decisions.

Signed _____

Pastor's Signature _____

Today's Date _____

ICC Authorized Signature and Date _____

> *We share together in the work of Jesus Christ, and, above all else, seek to encourage each other in doing his will. We will do our best to create an environment reflecting God's peace. (Phil 4:4–7) and be known by our love for one another. (2 Cor 8:24)*

SHARED RESPONSIBILITIES AMONG RESIDENT-CUSTODIANS

Each night

- Check all lights, including restrooms, baptistery, and lighted closets.
- Check all windows and doors. (The easiest way is to walk outside the building.)
- Sort mail.
- Throw out uncovered food.

Two or three times per week, depending on building use

- Clean all bathrooms (7): scrub toilets, sinks, floors, mirrors, shelves; "spot clean" stall doors and handles, room walls.
- Empty trash throughout building.
- Stock paper goods in bathrooms and sink areas.

Weekly

- Cleaning entire building.
- Put out trash for collection.
- Water all plants, pinch off brown leaves, wash underdishes.
- Eliminate clutter throughout building: basement hallway, tabletops, counters, corners. This is a judgment call, but do the best you can.
- Maintain utility room.

Sunday night

- Check all worship areas for technology turned off, windows locked, doors locked, candles cold, clutter.

Bimonthly

- Clean grease tank.

As needed

- Change lightbulbs.
- Order supplies (check with property care team first).
- Scrub trash cans.
- Outside yard: mow, rake, sweep steps and sidewalks, shovel and de-ice sidewalks and walkways.
- Sweep roof over Killam Hall.
- Two times a year (June/November) clean low gutters.
- Projects as requested by ICC.

Liability Waiver

I hereby release International Community Church, an American Baptist Church, of all liability in the event of any accident or injury to my person or property during or related to my cleaning of the church building.

Signed _____
Resident-Custodian's Signature

Signed _____
ICC Authorized Signature

Today's Date _____

Appendix C

Poems by Jack Powers

INSTRUCT ME
2/28/2000

That I might bear the burden,
Instruct me, that I may serve.

ARTIFACT
2/28/2000

Nonetheless beauteous
despite the malformed skeleton
and the imperfect fleshy layerings,
the Guest that you urgently seek
is there, beneath the artiface.
Under the least rock God's Spirit lives,
Kneel, and dig, this is asked of you.

REWARD

2/27/1999 (For Juliet)

And when we are called,
and the final trumpet blown,
the craven and heroes, alike,
will pass through Heaven's door,
the craven, to be released
from the multiple burdens of Earth,
But, the heroes, to see the seeds,
so earnestly, and persistently sown,
aweave and blossoming,
in the Creator's Valley,
fully grown.

Bibliography

Miller, Holly G. *Sustaining Pastoral Excellence: A Progress Report on a Lilly Endowment Initiative.* Indianapolis, IN: Lilly Endowment, 2011. http://www.pastoralexcellence.com/pdfs/Final_SPE_Report2011.pdf.

Young, William Paul. *The Shack.* Newbury Park, CA: Windblown Media, 2008.

www.ingramcontent.com/pod-product-compliance
Lightning Source LLC
Chambersburg PA
CBHW051107160426
43193CB00010B/1349